Emotional Intelligence Works

Works

Developing "People Smart" Strategies

Revised Edition

S. Michael Kravitz, Ph.D.
Susan D. Schubert, M.A.

A Crisp Fifty-Minute™ Series Book

Emotional Intelligence Works

Developing "People Smart" Strategies

Revised Edition

S. Michael Kravitz, Ph.D.
Susan D. Schubert, M.A.

CREDITS:

VP Product Development:	**Matt Gambino**
Editor:	**Robb Tillett**
Production Editor:	**Genevieve McDermott**
Production Artists:	**Nicole Phillips and Betty Hopkins**

Trademarks

Crisp Fifty-Minute Series is a trademark of Axzo Press.

Some of the product names and company names used in this book have been used for identification purposes only and may be trademarks or registered trademarks of their respective manufacturers and sellers.

Disclaimer

We reserve the right to revise this publication and make changes from time to time in its content without notice.

ISBN 10: 1-4260-9112-5
ISBN 13: 978-1-4260-9112-4
Library of Congress Catalog Card Number 2008937175
Printed in the United States of America
1 2 3 4 5 09 08

Learning Objectives for

EMOTIONAL INTELLIGENCE WORKS

The learning objectives for *Emotional Intelligence Works* are listed below. They have been developed to guide the user to the core issues covered in this book.

The objectives of this book are to help the user:

1) Explore the benefits and challenges of applying emotional intelligence

2) Obtain tools for assessing individual and organizational strengths and opportunities for improvement

3) Learn the core skills needed for emotional intelligence

4) Understand model strategies and examples for applying emotional intelligence in business and social settings, with family and friends

Assessing Progress

We have developed a Crisp Series **assessment** that covers the fundamental information presented in this book. A 25-item, multiple-choice and true/false questionnaire allows the reader to evaluate his or her comprehension of the subject matter.

To download the assessment and answer key, go to www.axzopress.com and search on the book title.

Assessments should not be used in any employee-selection process.

Preface

Consider how difficult it is to resolve a frustrating conflict caused by misunderstanding, poor timing, or inattentiveness. Because we rely so much on technology, and "virtual" everything, we may risk short-cutting or even ignoring our personal interactions.

As a consequence, we sometimes find ourselves in a timeless, placeless, faceless and very confusing environment, wasting time and losing the creativity that emerges from synergistic interactions with diverse people. At the moment, we cannot predict what new technologies will be available in the next decades to make our interactions both faster as well as more challenging. However, we can predict that there will be an increase in diversity among people from different cultures, countries, generations and abilities, all of whom will be requiring better communications skills.

To overcome the potential consequences of lost business and damaged relationships caused by inadequate communications, this newly-revised edition of "Emotional Intelligence Works" provides you with interpersonal tools to become more effective and successful in all your interactions (face-to-face and virtual) at school, in the community, at home, and in your workplace.

Research shows that the relationships most affected or afflicted by inadequate people skills include the following: supervisor to the people who report to him or her; one associate to another; customers to employees. All these relationships depend on your ability to interact effectively one-on-one, remotely, digitally, and in groups. While factual knowledge and how-to skills continue to be important, emotional and social intelligence skills have become even more crucial and valuable. The combination of intellectual knowledge and technical skills alone are insufficient for success in life.

During the past years since the first edition of *Emotional Intelligence Works*, we have applied the content in hundreds of different settings including schools and universities, government, non-profits, professional organizations, associations, hospitals, nursing homes, mental health centers, and various businesses. Now, we are using the results of our experiences as well as current research to update this book.

In this edition we are making a few modifications, including the following:

➤ Social intelligence has been incorporated into the book based on Daniel Goleman's recent book, *Social Intelligence* (2006). He emphasizes that we are designed for sociability. Goleman claims that humans have a natural bias toward "empathy, cooperation, and altruism" if we develop our social intelligence. If we fail to do so, our interactions with others may have a toxic impact, both physically and psychologically.

➤ The business communications section applies social intelligence to in-person as well as technology-assisted interactions.

➤ The enhanced self assessments will help you determine where you are already doing well and what improvements need attention.

➤ The major enhancement to the first edition is the inclusion of diversity skills with emotional intelligence. As work-force demographics of U.S.-based as well as international companies change, everyone faces complex challenges with customers and associates. For example, a report by The Novations Group Research on the relationship between diversity and the visual interpretation of emotions emphasizes the importance of adapting across cultures.

People who are not emotionally smart may waste time on personality conflicts and complaining. They may lose self-control when faced with tense and stressful situations, thus failing to attain their desired outcomes. Unsmart people undermine their own and others' performance and work satisfaction. Therefore, we are dedicated to helping you use this book to enhance your own skills as well as to become a role model for others.

Envision yourself on a mission to transform unsmart behaviors into productive approaches, enabling everyone to achieve greater satisfaction and become more successful.

About the Authors

Susan Schubert and Dr. Michael Kravitz are principals with Schubert-Kravitz Associates and Diversity Matters, LLP. Both firms are located in Ohio and are dedicated to improving emotional intelligence, diversity competence plus teamwork. The firms work with organizations that want to use the wisdom, creativity, and gifts of everyone to achieve individual and organizational as well as community success.

S. Michael Kravitz, Ph.D.

Dr. Kravitz is a speaker and educator. He provides practical, positive tools for building communication skills, overcoming negativity, dealing with difficult students, patients, and associates as well as raising emotional intelligence in the workplace. His keynote speeches and training programs are known for their high-content level and humor. He is an adjunct professor at Franklin University and author of the Crisp Series book, *Managing Negative People*. He received a B.S. in Education and both an M.A. and Ph.D. in Psychology from The Ohio State University.

Susan D. Schubert, M.A.

Susan Schubert builds group harmony through teamwork, solving problems, and increasing leadership skills. Schubert is a facilitator and trainer with an M.A. in Public Administration and Community Leadership from Central Michigan University. Group facilitation and team simulations for meetings, teams, and retreats are her strengths. She is co-author of the Crisp Series book, *Managing Upward*. She is active with community organizations and founded a women's interfaith group.

About This Book

Emotional Intelligence Works: Developing "People Smart" Strategies will help anyone learn how to succeed in interpersonal relationships—including front-line employees, supervisors, and business owners. The book provides guidelines on how to manage emotions, communicate intelligently, and raise your level of emotional intelligence in a constructive manner.

The easy-to-apply explanations, universal examples, exercises, and self-assessments provide opportunities to learn alone or in a group of associates within an organization. The reader can choose sections of the book that are of greatest interest and proceed at his or her own pace. Groups can select sections for improving teamwork. Managers will find guidance for training staff as well as improving their own leadership skills. Trainers may use the book as a course outline and workbook for all learners. The book is organized as follows:

Introduction

Includes an example of emotional intelligence, what it means, why it is important, and a self-assessment tool.

Part 1: "Think Smart" Strategies

"Think Smart" Strategies focus on understanding yourself and managing your emotions and thoughts in a variety of challenging situations. Smart thinking is the basis for smart actions and communications with others. Content includes strategies for understanding emotions and thoughts as well as becoming more empathetic and optimistic.

Part 2: "Be Smart" Strategies

"Be Smart" Strategies concentrate on actions you can take to be wiser in handling social interactions, managing change, and being more flexible. Smart actions make the difference between successful and unsuccessful interpersonal relationships. Content includes using social skills, becoming more flexible, and using coping skills. In addition, the following topics have been incorporated into the content: social intelligence and diversity.

Part 3: "Work Smart" Strategies

"Work Smart" Strategies are directed toward creating organizations in which emotionally smart people can be successful. Content includes conducting an organizational self-assessment, providing social skills training, fostering teamwork, and building passionate enthusiasm for work.

Table of Contents

INTRODUCTION

What Emotional Intelligence Means

Emotional Intelligence

The ability to use your emotions in a positive and constructive way in relationships with others.

Emotional intelligence is one of several types of intelligence required for success in all kinds of situations. People have different abilities in dealing with emotions just like they have different abilities in language, logic, mathematics, and music.

Sam is 70 years old. He still gets around pretty well and is able to handle the details of his life, including his banking. Unfortunately, Sam is a little hard to understand because his voice is harsh and gravelly. He sounds like he has something wrong with his vocal chords.

One Monday morning, Sam went to the bank to get some cash. He asked the teller to give him cash with his credit card. The teller spoke loudly to Sam (apparently assuming he was deaf because his speech was hard to understand). She said that she didn't understand what he wanted and that his credit card had expired. Then Sam spoke loudly to her and said he needed $50 in cash. By this time, everyone in the bank, including the security guard, was watching and listening. Both Sam and the teller were very frustrated, and Sam was obviously embarrassed.

The customer behind Sam went to the manager and quietly explained the situation. The manager joined the discussion and calmly invited Sam to come into his office to take care of his problem. In a few minutes, Sam was smiling and explaining what he needed. The teller returned to the rest of the customers and diplomatically apologized for keeping them waiting. Once everyone started using emotional intelligence, then business returned to normal.

In the article, "Promoting Social and Emotional Learning," Maurice J. Elias and others say that emotional intelligence is the ability to understand and express your emotions to meet the requirements of day-to-day living, learning, and relating to others. It is important to use emotional intelligence because it will help you to:

➤ Solve problems by using both logic and feelings.

➤ Be flexible in changing situations.

➤ Help other people express their needs.

➤ Calmly and thoughtfully respond to difficult people.

➤ Keep an optimistic and positive outlook.

➤ Express empathy, compassion, and caring for others.

Continuously learn how to improve yourself and your organization. Enhance your interactions and communications with those from other cultures.

The Need for "People Smart" Strategies

Today, our lives are filled with change and "busy-ness" at home and at work. When the pace of life was slower and more predictable, it was easier to be pleasant, calm, peaceful, and thoughtful. The old expectations about work relationships just do not apply anymore.

You have to figure out how to interact with people in new and different ways because:

> ➤ The variety of people you deal with everyday challenges you to be flexible, kind, and adaptive in your communications.

> ➤ Constant pressure and stress make you tired and irritable so that it is hard to stay calm and thoughtful.

> ➤ An increasing number of employees believe they have less control over their work and their lives than they did in the past. They complain and express pessimism about their future.

> ➤ Instead of learning these skills from positive role models in the family, many organizations have to teach people how to communicate respectfully to their associates and customers.

> ➤ Rude behavior at work is on the rise. Some blame the increase on the "lean-and-mean" trend toward doing more with less. More demands on fewer employees have led to unchecked incivility and less caring for others.

Daniel Goleman, author of *Emotional Intelligence*, claims, "Emotional-intelligence-based capabilities are twice as important for star performance as IQ and technical skills combined."

Research indicates that the biggest reason that managers fail is poor interpersonal skills. According to The Center for Creative Leadership in Greensboro, North Carolina, roughly half of all managers have problems relating to their associates and employees.

Assess Your Emotional Intelligence

Improve your emotional intelligence skills through objective assessment, learning, and practice—the same way you would improve skills in mathematics, language, sports, or music. Start your personal improvement plan by assessing your current level of emotional intelligence. Use the following four-step process.

Step 1: Prepare Yourself

Respond to the questions on the following page by being honest and objective about what you actually do now. Choose a focus such as "on-the-job," "with your family," or "on a non-profit board of trustees."

Or, have another person complete the questions based on his or her observations of you. Select someone who knows you well and whom you trust to give you objective, helpful feedback. This person could be your immediate supervisor, a business associate, or a team member. Select a spouse or close friend to complete the assessment if you wish to increase emotional intelligence in your personal life.

Step 2: Complete the Assessment

Be as honest and objective as you can when you respond to the following statements. Do you believe that you do the following things more than 75% of the time? If you agree, circle "YES."

1. I am aware when I start to become angry or defensive.   Yes

2. When I am dealing with others' anger, I keep relaxed and goal-oriented.   Yes

3. I remain cheerful and enjoy working with new ideas.   Yes

4. I follow through on assignments, support others, and build trust.   Yes

5. Despite setbacks and problems, I continue to work on projects in a calm manner.   Yes

6. I use positive thinking even when I am in a conflict or in a difficult situation.   Yes

7. I can feel and "see" things from another person's viewpoint.   Yes

8. Before I make a decision or take an action, I listen to others' ideas.   Yes

9. When I communicate with others, I help them feel good.   Yes

10. To resolve conflicts, I encourage honest and respectful discussion.   Yes

11. I help people who hold different opinions to reach agreement.   Yes

12. When I am making changes, I consider the feelings of others.   Yes

13. I am aware of when I start to use negative thinking.   Yes

14. I practice stress management to be calm and healthy.   Yes

15. I have a good sense of humor.   Yes

Step 3: Score the Assessment

How many times did you circle "YES"? _____

The overall assessment of your current emotional intelligence is as follows:

13-15 = Very high

10-12 = High

7-9 = Average

4-6 = Below average

1-3 = Far below average

Step 4: Assess Your Current Strengths and Weaknesses

Each of the 15 statements listed in the assessment on the previous page reflects your emotional skill level in one of five emotional intelligence skill categories: Self-Awareness, Social Skills, Optimism, Emotional Control, and Flexibility. To interpret your score in each group, match each "YES" you circled in the previous list with each Y in the following table. Be sure to circle each Y across the row for every statement.

For example, if you circled "YES" to Statement 2, then circle all Y's in that row. On the other hand, if you did not circle "YES" for 2, you would circle nothing in that row.

Five Emotional Intelligence Skills

Statement Number	Self-Awareness	Social Skills	Optimism	Emotional Control	Flexibility
1	Y				
2	Y	Y		Y	Y
3			Y	Y	
4	Y	Y	Y		
5	Y		Y	Y	Y
6	Y		Y	Y	Y
7		Y			
8		Y	Y	Y	Y
9		Y	Y		Y
10	Y	Y		Y	Y
11		Y		Y	Y
12	Y	Y			
13	Y		Y		Y
14				Y	
15			Y		
Skill Total					
Interpretation					

Review your results for each set of skills. For example, if you scored 8 for self-awareness, then your interpretation is very high for that skill. Write your interpretation in the last row under each skill.

Interpretation

8 = Very high   6-7 = High   4-5 = Average
2-3 = Below average   0-1 = Far below average

Five Emotional Intelligence Skills

The five emotional intelligence skills are a combination of several researchers' work on emotional intelligence. Following is a summary of the five skills. There are detailed explanations, strategies, examples, and learning tools in the rest of this book.

Self-Awareness Skills (see Parts 1 and 3)
Emotionally intelligent people are aware of how they feel, what motivates and de-motivates them, and how they affect others.

Social Skills (see Parts 2 and 3)
Emotionally intelligent people communicate and relate well with others. They listen intently and adapt their communications to others' unique needs, including diverse backgrounds. They show compassion.

Optimism (see Parts 1 and 3)
Emotionally intelligent people have a positive and optimistic outlook on life. Their mental attitude energizes them to work steadily towards goals despite setbacks.

Emotional Control (see Parts 1 and 3)
Emotionally intelligent people handle stress evenly. They deal calmly with emotionally stressful situations such as change and interpersonal conflicts.

Flexibility Skills (see Parts 2 and 3)
Emotionally intelligent people adapt to changes. They use problem-solving to develop options.

PREPARE TO IMPROVE YOUR
EMOTIONAL INTELLIGENCE SKILLS

If you completed the self-assessment alone, respond to the following:

My best emotional intelligence skills are
(select skills with a "high" or "very high" rating):

_____

_____

_____

_____

My emotional intelligence skills most in need of improvement are
(select skills with a "below average" or "far below average" rating):

_____

_____

_____

_____

The emotional intelligence skills that are most important for me to improve are:

_____

_____

_____

_____

CONTINUED

If you and another person completed your self-assessment, schedule a meeting to discuss the result. Use the spaces below to record your discussion.

The emotional intelligence skills that we both rate "high" or "very high" for me are:

_____

_____

_____

_____

The emotional intelligence skills that we both rate "below average" or "far below average" are:

_____

_____

_____

_____

The emotional intelligence skills that are most important for me to improve are:

_____

_____

_____

_____

"Think Smart" Strategies

Making the Choice to Think Wisely

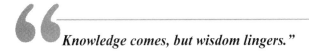

Knowledge comes, but wisdom lingers."

–Alfred Lord Tennyson

Some people say that thinking is what makes us human. Which comes first: thinking or feeling or acting? The premise of emotional intelligence is that humans can make choices about what they say and do. It is possible to control the way you think about and react to crises and to daily stresses. It is possible to use your entire brain (including your emotions) to make wise decisions.

Ten-year-old Elana says that being smart with people means thinking before you talk and while talking. You also have to think about what you have said after you finish talking. What does Elana think about? She says, "I think 'I can do it.' I am self-confident."

How does all this thinking help? If she does not think first, Elana says, "my mind goes kerplink." This means blank or confused. If she thinks before she speaks, she says, "I can do better things and be more creative."

Thinking Smart

The benefits of learning how to think wisely:

➤ You will make better decisions and avoid saying and doing things that you will regret later.

➤ You will have less stress in your life and cause less stress for others.

➤ You will achieve more positive outcomes.

The challenges to thinking smart:

➤ Reacting automatically

➤ Thinking pessimistically

Two strategies for meeting the thinking smart challenges:

➤ Become more self-aware by understanding your thoughts and motivators.

➤ Become more optimistic to improve your thinking.

Strategy 1: Self-Awareness Skills

In *Emotional Intelligence*, Daniel Goleman says that self-awareness—the ability to recognize a feeling as it happens—is the keystone of emotional intelligence. Self-awareness is clarity about your feelings and thoughts. With awareness comes the ability to make better choices.

Self-Awareness Skill Builder 1: Understand Your Brain

Your brain has three parts that work together like a team of advisors. The three parts are instinct, emotions, and logic. Their goal is to keep you safe and give you advice. Each advisor has a different set of skills. Sometimes they give you conflicting advice and sometimes they are silent. Your job is to learn how to hear all three advisors and make the best choices based on their combined input.

The best way to understand how the three advisors work is to see them in action in a real situation.

> Susan returned home alone after a late-night meeting. She pulled into the garage, got out of the car and walked around to go inside. A person in a ski mask jumped out of the bushes, ran over to her, pointed a gun in her face and said, "Gimme your purse." How should Susan use her advisors to decide what to do?

Advisors	Their Skills	Their Strengths	Their Weaknesses	Their Interactions
Instinct	Identifies danger. Will advise you whether to fight back or run away.	Gets you to act fast without thinking.	May get you to act too quickly and dangerously without conscious thought.	Can be silenced by the other advisors especially when they join forces.
Emotions	Uses your memories and what you have learned in the past.	Helps you to make decisions based on your feelings about past experiences and learning.	May draw the wrong conclusions about a situation.	Can be silenced by the other advisors especially when they join forces.
Logic	Thoroughly analyzes problems and comes up with options.	Will help you to carefully consider logical options. Helps you to prepare for the future.	May need time and accurate information to thoroughly consider all options.	Can be silenced by the other advisors especially when they join forces.

Remember, guidance from one advisor can be silenced by other advisors. For example, when the advisors of instinct and emotions shout at you, it is impossible to hear the advisor of logic.

Thinking smart requires being aware of, and listening to, all three advisors carefully. Planning and preparation is one of the best ways to intentionally use the best advice from all of your advisors.

Self-Awareness Skill Builder 2: Hear Yourself Think

How do you react when you are in a crisis? In an emergency, it is especially difficult to hear from the "advisor of logic." Most people respond to "gut feelings" which are a combination of advice from the advisors of instinct and emotions. Without the balance of all three, there is danger of making a less-effective decision.

In the example of the masked gunman with the ski mask, Susan could have mentally rehearsed what she would do in the event she would be held up in a variety of situations. Her logical brain might have prepared her to protect herself first and her property second.

Although most people rarely face life-threatening situations, the everyday wear-and-tear of tight time schedules, irritable people, and personal problems requires clear thinking. Everyone has periodic crises that make it even more difficult to stay calm and clear-headed. The frequency and extent of crises depend on the kind of work you do and on personal circumstances.

What kind of crises and daily stresses do you experience? Which of these stressors happen repeatedly?

❏ Managing an overloaded work schedule

❏ Personal or family illness

❏ Demanding customers

❏ Numerous and unpredictable changes

❏ Financial struggles

❏ Responsibility for children or aging parents

❏ Other:

Self-Awareness Skill Builder 3: Stop Responding Automatically

Start taking control of the way you think and act by listening to your own emotions and thoughts. Find out why you react the way you do to crises and stress. Learn more about yourself. Mentally prepare yourself for improving how to think and respond in the future.

Four Techniques for Learning About Yourself

1. Relax.

2. Catch yourself thinking.

3. Find the causes.

4. Understand what motivates you.

Technique 1: Relax

Relaxation helps your mind feel more at peace so that you can think clearly. When you feel peaceful, you are aware of what is happening with your emotions, body, and mind. People in the grip of a very strong emotion such as anger or fear find it difficult to be emotionally aware.

Slow down your breathing. Take a deep breath and let it out slowly. Breathe deeply a few times. Become aware of your feelings, thoughts, and responses. Allow your body to relax. Tense and relax your muscles. Let the knots out of your cramped muscles. Breathe slowly and gently.

In your new state of relaxation, revisit the event that caused you to become very upset. Remember what happened. It could have been a customer cursing at you, a driver cutting you off, your spouse accusing you of something you didn't do, or a co-worker who lied about you.

Describing the Event

I am really upset about (describe situation or event) _____

_____

Technique 2: Catch Yourself Thinking

Now, remember how you felt and what you thought when the event happened. Accept and describe your feelings and thoughts. Once you have fully analyzed your emotions, you will be able to direct your new thinking into wiser actions.

Ask yourself, "What did my body tell me about how I felt? Where did I feel tense? Hands, arms, back, neck, or stomach? Did I have a headache? Was my gut reaction to fight or flee? Was I so angry that I thought about how to get even with that person?"

Identifying your Reactions

When I think about that situation, I remember that I felt _____

_____

I remember at the time, I thought _____

_____

Technique 3: Find the Causes

Uncover the true causes for your strong reactions such as anger, revenge, fear, sorrow, or exhaustion. Be aware that the true causes may not be immediately obvious to you. Search deeply for the truth to find the hidden meanings. Imagine that you are peeling away the layers of an onion by using questions (who, what, why, when, how) to uncover the hidden layers of meaning.

Why were you angry or afraid? Were you frustrated because someone or something got in the way of your goals? What old feelings came back from your childhood or a previous job? When were your beliefs or values compromised? Why did you find the person's words or actions offensive to you? When do you usually get upset?

Go deeper into your own difficult situation to find the underlying causes. Use the "why" technique by asking yourself several times:

"Why do I feel upset when _____ happens?"

Keep asking and answering questions until you believe you have peeled away the truth about your emotions.

Technique 4: Understand What Motivates You

The underlying cause of your responses relates to what motivates you. Motivation is why people do what they do. Motivation is like the fuel that powers an automobile. It is the energy-source that affects how you make decisions and respond to interpersonal challenges. Once you know what kind of "fuel" drives you, it is possible to improve your thinking and make better choices.

Do you know what motivates you?

Self-Awareness Skill Builder: 4: Use The STEP Model

One way to find out what motivates you is to use the STEP Model. This approach provides a way to help you understand what conditions positively and negatively affect your thoughts. By becoming aware of how you think, you will be able to listen to your personal advisors and make better decisions. The table in the assessment on the next page provides an opportunity to select words and phrases that describe how you communicate in different situations.

Use the STEP model to help you to:

➤ Understand what motivates you in different situations.

➤ Use words to describe how you are in those situations.

➤ Use your self-awareness to hear your personal advisors and make better choices.

STEP Self-Assessment

Select a situation as the focus for your self-assessment. For example, work situations might be handling customers on the telephone or leading a team or teaching a skill.

Situation: _____

Now select and circle a total of five words or phrases from all columns that best describe the way you communicate in that situation. Any combination is possible including the selection of all five words in one column.

S	T	E	P
Stable	Thorough	Emotional	Pusher
Cooperative	Questioning	Outgoing	Assertive
Specialist	Perfectionist	People oriented	Controlling
Laid Back	Unemotional	Talkative	Quick
Feeling secure	Doing things right	Being liked	Getting results

Total the number of items (phrases or words) you circled in each of the four columns. Place the totals in the corresponding boxes below.

Highlight the column with the highest total points, or select the two columns that are tied for the highest point totals. For example, if you had a total of 3 under the E column, then E would be your communication style. If you had a total of 2 for both the S and T columns, they are your two strongest styles for the specific situation you identified. If you have high scores in two categories, you have a combination communication style.

Motivators and Warning Signs

Each letter (STEP) at the top of each column has a meaning. The first word after each letter names the style.

S = Stable	T = Thorough	E = Emotional	P = Pusher

The words you selected are general descriptions of how you are in the specific situation and may not apply elsewhere. If you chose a work situation, you may not be the same way at home.

The table on the following page shows the relationship between each STEP style and emotionally intelligent thinking.

Emotionally Intelligent Thinking: Description of how you think, feel, and communicate in situations that are motivating and positive.

Motivators: Situations that tend to be most satisfying and stimulating to you.

De-motivators: Situations that tend to be irritating and annoying and cause you to disconnect from all your advisors, especially the logical advisor.

Danger Signs: These are warning signals that describe your emotions and thoughts when you are reacting automatically. These danger signs are a reminder to slow down and think carefully.

Motivators and Warning Signs

STEP Style	
Stable	**Emotionally Intelligent Thinking:** You tend to think carefully and follow detailed steps. Your emotions are calm and quiet as you work steadily at getting the job done. **Motivators:** A predictable situation with slow, limited change. Working in a small team with people you know well. Having standard procedures. Knowing what is expected. Positive relationships. **De-motivators:** Rapid and unpredictable change. Unclear expectations. No procedures to follow. Unfriendly atmosphere. **Danger Signs:** You tend to become confused and uncertain, believe people don't appreciate you. Your feelings are easily hurt. You think about getting even.
Thorough	**Emotionally Intelligent Thinking:** You tend to think logically and analytically, ask a lot of questions of yourself and others. **Motivators:** A situation that values precision, accuracy, and logic. Creating and following guidelines to produce excellent results. **De-motivators:** Chaotic, confusing work environment where tasks need to be completed quickly without regard for quality standards. **Danger Signs:** You may become critical of yourself and others. Find mistakes and faults with everything.
Emotional	**Emotionally Intelligent Thinking:** You tend to react to feelings, be sensitive to your own and others' emotions. **Motivators:** A situation in which you use your interpersonal communication skills. Being liked and asked to help. **De-motivators:** Working alone—little contact with people. Lots of conflict and arguments. People who disregard your feelings. **Danger Signs:** May believe that people don't like you. Worry about losing relationships. Exaggerate your emotional responses without logic.
Pusher	**Emotionally Intelligent Thinking:** You tend to think fast and act fast. Can make fast decisions under stress. **Motivators:** A situation in which you can get things done quickly. Being in control. Lots of opportunity for change. Seeing results of your efforts. **De-motivators:** Situations in which there is no chance for control. Getting slowed down by lots of details. **Danger Signs:** May become frustrated with others who waste time. May jump to quick conclusions. You may demand that people do things your way.

Use a New Mental Script

Change the way you think about challenging situations by using your logical advisors and your understanding of the STEP model. When you begin to experience warning signs, pause to understand what you are thinking and feeling, listen to all your advisors, remember how you prepared yourself for the situation. Develop a new mental script.

Helpful Questions

What was an example of your most emotionally challenging situation? (For example, preparing for a new computer system in your office or getting married to someone who has three children from a previous marriage.)

_____

_____

_____

What did you think and feel when that happened? (For example, I was anxious and uncertain.)

_____

_____

_____

What can you do to help yourself stay calm, relaxed, and hear yourself thinking? (Think about the situation during a quiet and peaceful time. Anticipate likely situations.)

_____

_____

_____

Revise Your Thoughts

Example of emotionally intelligent thinking: "*Even though the situation is chaotic and unclear right now, I know I can do things to improve. I need to stay positive and stop complaining about what I cannot control. I can pinpoint specifically what is upsetting me by understanding my STEP style. I can take some actions that will help me to stay calm.*"

If my style is…

> ➤ **Stable:** I may be feeling de-motivated because I have no idea what is expected of me. I will gather as much information as possible in order to be flexible to the changes. I must accept the fact that the way I do things may change and my routine isn't what it has been.

> ➤ **Thorough:** I may be irritated by the confusion and conflict, this may be just my opportunity to research how other people adapted to similar changes.

> ➤ **Emotional:** I am concerned about damaging friendly relationships with my associates or family. I will make sure I keep up my other friendships. For example, with my special friends at work, I will make arrangements to stay in touch outside of work time.

> ➤ **Pusher:** I may be frustrated because I can't reach my own goals. I need to look around and listen to people to find out their goals. I will slow down a bit and accept that there will be some time before the direction is totally clear. It is important that I stop trying to control everyone and everything.

For the Future

What can you do to prepare yourself mentally and emotionally next time an emotionally challenging situation happens?

_____

_____

How can you use the STEP model?

_____

_____

Strategy 2: Optimistic Thinking

Optimism contributes to emotional intelligence and job success in the workplace. Most smart people have a positive outlook on life. They have high levels of happiness and energy. Emotionally smart people feel that they are important and the work they do is valuable. Because they are optimistic, they have energy to work steadily towards goals despite crises.

Are You a Pessimist?

If you are a pessimist, you may view the world as dangerous and likely to get worse. You probably dedicate much of your thinking to worrying and expecting the worst.

Are You an Optimist?

Do you see the world as positive, safe, and enjoyable? If so, you probably dedicate your thinking to solving problems and finding new approaches.

Optimism Builder 1: Determine How Optimistic or Pessimistic You Are

Complete the optimism quiz that follows. If a statement describes the way you act or think more than half the time, circle T. Otherwise, circle F.

TRUE OR FALSE?

		T	F
1.	I think more about coming up with solutions than worrying about why they won't work.	❏	❏
2.	People need to prove themselves before I trust them.	❏	❏
3.	I enjoy the challenges of my job.	❏	❏
4.	I feel that what I do helps others.	❏	❏
5.	I am able to "laugh" at myself.	❏	❏
6.	I have a good sense of humor.	❏	❏
7.	I don't trust anyone or anything.	❏	❏
8.	I seldom take breaks from work.	❏	❏
9.	I take at least one day off each week (one day out of seven).	❏	❏
10.	I enjoy encouraging, supporting, and helping others succeed.	❏	❏
11.	I trust people unless they show me they can't be trusted.	❏	❏
12.	I have difficulty saying that I can't take on another responsibility.	❏	❏
13.	I feel like I seldom have time for myself.	❏	❏
14.	I work at developing positive and supportive friendships.	❏	❏
15.	I put up with people who are negative.	❏	❏
16.	I am happy and cheerful.	❏	❏
17.	I eat a healthful diet (avoid excessive amounts of fat, sugar and stimulants).	❏	❏
18.	I engage in active exercise for 20 minutes a day at least three times a week (if my health permits).	❏	❏
19.	I feel tired most days.	❏	❏
20.	I usually have short periods throughout the day when I "nod off."	❏	❏
21.	I engage in daily meditation or relaxation exercises.	❏	❏

ANSWER KEY: TRUE OR FALSE?

Match your responses from the optimism quiz to the list below. Circle the matching responses. For example, if you circled T for #1, circle 1 below. If you circled F for #1, there is no match.

T: The following numbers are True:

1   3   4   5   6   9   10   11   14   16   17   18   21

F: The following numbers are False:

2   7   8   12   13   15   19   20

How many total matches did you circle? _____

Interpret the Optimism Quiz

19-21 matches: **Model optimist.** You are exceptional! You can be a role model to help others become more positive.

13-18 matches: **Usually optimistic.** Keep up the good work. You are optimistic and may not need much development.

6-12 matches: **Sometimes optimistic.** You can improve your emotional intelligence by developing your optimistic outlook on life.

0-5 matches: **Seldom Optimistic.** Unless you develop your optimism, your emotional intelligence is likely to remain at a low level.

Optimism Builder 2: Talk to Yourself Differently

Become more optimistic by gradually changing your beliefs. Which of the following do you believe?

"It makes no difference what I do because bad things will happen to me anyway!"

or

"The actions that I take can make a difference. I can make things better."

People with the first set of beliefs tell themselves that other people and circumstances rule their lives. Pessimistic self-talk may cause people to give up without even trying to initiate changes. When faced with challenges, negative thinkers may say, "I can't. I won't. Why should I even try? It won't make a difference, anyway. They won't let me. It's their fault that I have these problems."

People with the second set of beliefs have confidence that they can control *some* aspects of their lives. Positive thinking leads people to take action even when they have problems. When faced with challenges, optimistic people may think, "I will try. It does matter what I do. I can make a difference. I can take responsibility for improving things." Positive and optimistic thinking is more likely than negative thinking to lead to successful outcomes.

Practice Becoming More Positive

What are you really telling yourself about a problem that needs to be solved or a change that needs to be made? Gradually change what you are saying to yourself. Start with a pessimistic, negative statement then change it step-by-step to positive and optimistic thinking.

Most pessimistic and negative statement...

"I can't do anything about _____. It won't matter what I try to do. There's no point in even trying."

Improved statement...

"I might be able to do something about _____. There may be some small things that I can do to make things better."

Even more optimistic statement...

"I will do something positive about _____. In the past, I was able to do something similar and it made a difference."

Most positive and optimistic statement...

"I'm convinced that I can turn these problems with _____ into challenges that I will be able to meet. I have the skills, information, and help that I need to make a difference."

Follow Up

As you gradually work toward your goal, keep your revised statement near you and look at it frequently. A mental shift can affect your perspective about your work.

Optimism Builder 3: See Meaning in Your Work

> ❝ *Everybody must have meaning in his life… A long life isn't necessarily a happy life."*

–Mr. Karma Ura, head of the Center for Bhutan Studies

People who believe their work is important usually feel more positive than those who believe their work is meaningless. Some people find meaning in their work by helping others, developing new products or ideas, stimulating their minds, making money for their family, bringing about social changes or learning new skills.

Concentrate on what is important to you about your job. Try to do more of what is meaningful to you. If you find there is *nothing* satisfying about your work, then no amount of mental control will change it. Consider looking for a new job or a new career.

The work that I do is important because _____

_____

I especially enjoy what I do because _____

_____

Optimism Builder 4: Care for Yourself and Others

Optimistic people often develop trusting relationships that serve as mutual support networks. Since work life and home life often overlap, people need to develop a network of positive, supportive people in both places. Smart people actively seek out positive people at work and at home.

A supportive network may provide you with some or all of the following benefits:

➤ Be available to help with problem solving.

➤ Share information that might be helpful.

➤ Warn you about problems.

➤ Help you feel better about yourself and recognize your achievements.

➤ Have fun together.

➤ Be a supportive friend.

IDENTIFY YOUR SUPPORT NETWORK

Chances are you already have a network of supportive friends, family, or co-workers. Consider who the people are in your network and write their names here.

Who is your support team at home?

_____

_____

What does each one do to help you?

_____

_____

How do you help them?

_____

_____

Who is on your support team at work?

_____

_____

What does each one do to help you?

_____

_____

How do you help them?

_____

_____

How do you let them know how much you appreciate them?

_____

_____

"Think Smart" Summary

An Action Plan for Using "Think Smart" People Strategies

Review the Think Smart Strategies for improving interpersonal relationships. Fill in the action steps you will take to become emotionally intelligent as you think about how you respond to others.

Strategy 1: Self-awareness skills include...

> ➤ Understanding how and why you think and react

> ➤ How to respond thoughtfully to emotional challenges by hearing yourself think

> ➤ Understanding what motivates you

The steps I plan to take to improve my self-awareness skills are:

_____

_____

_____

_____

Strategy 2: Optimistic thinking comes from...

> ➤ Talking positively to yourself

> ➤ Seeing meaning and value in your work

> ➤ Having a support network

> ➤ Caring about and helping others

The steps I plan to take to become more optimistic are:

_____

_____

_____

_____

P A R T 2

"Be Smart"
Strategies

The Three Keys

> *We are wired to connect... our brain's very design makes it sociable... whenever we engage with another person."*

–*Social Intelligence* **by Daniel Goleman**

Opportunities for person to person connections decrease with the increased usage of modern technologies. In addition to our virtual relations, we need supportive and nourishing personal relationships.

In 2004, a survey of 2.5 billion televisions viewers in 72 countries showed that the average person spent 3 hours and 39 minutes watching television daily. However, television usage has been replaced by the Internet as the most common use of free time. In Goleman's book, Social Intelligence, he cites a startling statistic: "For every hour people spend using the Internet, their face-to-face contact with friends, coworkers, and the family fell by 24 minutes. You can't get a hug and a kiss over the Internet."

The quantities of our friendships and business connections are not as important as the quality of those interactions. Stressful relationships are linked to specific genes that help control the strength of our immune systems resulting in more frequent illness, both physical and mental. As Goleman notes, "nourishing relationships have a beneficial impact on our health, while toxic ones can act like slow poison in our bodies."

Emotionally intelligent people know how to be smart in their interactions with people. They adapt their words and actions to the needs of particular people in changing situations. They adapt to the communications needs of diverse people from different generations, countries of origin, ethnicity, religions, genders, and abilities.

The three keys to creating smart and beneficial relationships are:

➤ Using well-developed social skills to communicate effectively with others

➤ Being flexible to adapt when change happens

➤ Controlling one's emotions to deal with anger and cope with stress

➤ Showing kindness towards others

Strategy 1: Social Skills

In the past, people were measured by their education, experience, expertise, and knowledge…now people are judged by how well they handle themselves and interact with others, not just their intelligence and job skills. The ability to communicate feelings as well as facts makes the difference between success and failure in relating to others, particularly as demographic shifts affect our daily lives.

Communicate Effectively

The benefits of using social skills to communicate effectively are:

- ➤ You will feel more peaceful and relaxed.
- ➤ You can use your whole brain to make better choices.
- ➤ Others will understand you better.
- ➤ Your associates will consider your ideas and feelings in their decision-making.
- ➤ You will be a role model.
- ➤ Interpersonal communications will improve for everyone.
- ➤ The talents and wisdom of everyone in the group will be used more fully.

The challenges of using social skills to communicate effectively are:

- ➤ Not really listening
- ➤ Neglecting others' communication styles
- ➤ Giving up with those who are hard to understand
- ➤ Making assumptions about those who seem "different"

Social Skill Builder 1: Improve Your Listening Skills

Listening helps you understand how people feel and your attentiveness helps them express their thoughts and feelings to you. Careful listening shows that you care about and respect those around you. When people feel they are receiving respect and consideration, they are more likely to communicate calmly, clearly and sincerely.

ASSESS YOUR LISTENING EFFECTIVENESS

Read the following statements about effective listening. Then, check whether you do or do not practice these listening techniques most of the time. Be as honest and objective as you can. Adapt the statements to your situation.

	Yes	No
True listening comes from being focused and concentrating on the person with full attention.	❑	❑
It is respectful to show interest in the speaker by focusing with your eyes, ears, and your body even when you are talking on the telephone.	❑	❑
Frequent clock watching or electronic interruptions are distracting and may demonstrate unkindness.	❑	❑
Let the person know in advance how much time is available for a discussion.	❑	❑
Avoid completing paperwork or doing other things while they are talking.	❑	❑
Multi-tasking can result in misunderstandings and errors.	❑	❑
Restate in your own words what you think someone else is saying to get a clear understanding of his or her meaning.	❑	❑
Ask questions to clarify what a person is saying especially if there are challenges with accents or speech abilities.	❑	❑
Ask for clarification if you are not sure that you accurately understood the other person.	❑	❑
Use questions to show sincere interest in what the speaker is saying.	❑	❑
Start questions with *why, what, when, where, how, who.*	❑	❑
It is tempting to interrupt people when they ramble and repeat themselves. Instead, say something kind such as, "I am so sorry to interrupt. I really need to get to another meeting."	❑	❑
Gently help people to get to their point. For example, "I want to be absolutely sure that I understand your main point. Is this it…?"	❑	❑

CONTINUED

CONTINUED

	Yes	No

While listening, it may be difficult to think about what you want to say. Your reply will emerge naturally and honestly when you are truly present and focused in the moment. If you are unsure of your reply, say so and ask for time to think. ☐ ☐

Put everything unrelated to the current exchange out of your mind while communicating with a person. Many listeners use phrases or questions such as, "umm hmm, I'm listening, I understand." Better ways to show interest are to use questions related to what they are saying or to restate in your own words some key points they are making. ☐ ☐

Use spontaneous responses or even silence to show that you are listening. Eye contact and nodding provide silent cues that you are paying attention. ☐ ☐

Use the Results of Your Listening Assessment

If most of your responses are "Yes," then you are already an effective listener. Where you marked "No" select the statements and add your own strategies that you can use to improve your listening skills by completing the following sentence: "I can improve my listening skills by _____

_____ ."

Social Skill Builder 2:
Adapt to the Communication Needs of Others

The following table describes different communication styles as well as their strengths and potential weaknesses. Observe that people may use a combination of styles. As you read through the list, think about a person with whom you would like to improve your communication. Select the one or two styles that this person uses most frequently. Underline the words that best describe this person and check the strategies that are most likely to be successful.

STABLE	
Communication Strengths	**Possible Communication Weaknesses**
They are agreeable, cooperative, team players. Sensitive and empathetic to other peoples' feelings. Communicate well on-to-one and in small groups.	May get quiet and withdrawn during conflicts. Feelings may get hurt by how you talk to them. May resist or avoid change. Their motto is, "If it ain't broke, don't fix it."

Stable Communication Strategies
- ➤ Help them to feel safe and secure.
- ➤ Prepare them for change with details and clear goals.
- ➤ To facilitate complete understanding, ask open-ended questions.
- ➤ Give ongoing positive feedback.
- ➤ Appreciate their skills and contributions.
- ➤ Be courteous and respectful.
- ➤ Stay calm.
- ➤ Encourage them to express their feelings.
- ➤ Provide all the information they need to do their work.

THOROUGH	
Communication Strengths	**Possible Communication Weaknesses**
They are logical and analytical. Ask many questions. Organize tasks and projects to get them done well.	May be critical of themselves and others. May have trouble making decisions because they get bogged down in research. Tend to avoid dealing with peoples' feelings. Their motto is, "If you can't do it right, don't do it at all."

Thorough Communication Strategies

➤ Focus on quality results. Reassure them that a new approach will not lower quality or standards.

➤ Research your facts and statements before you talk to them.

➤ Use logical reasoning and data to support your conclusions.

➤ Explain that feelings are also important to getting quality results.

➤ Don't talk down to them.

➤ Recognize their expertise and analytical skills.

➤ Never challenge their expertise.

➤ Help them set realistic expectations for themselves and others so they can be efficient.

| EMOTIONAL ||
Communication Strengths	Possible Communication Weaknesses
They are friendly, talkative, outgoing, caring, and people-oriented. Persuade other people to work together and start new projects.	May be too concerned with feelings and not deal with business. Sometimes have trouble managing time because they're so busy talking. Have difficulty separating work issues from personal issues. Will avoid dealing with conflict because they don't want to hurt anyone's feelings. Their motto is, "Let's relax and have fun."

Emotional Communication Strategies

➤ Help them get organized.
➤ Appeal to their need to be accepted and liked.
➤ Avoid personal criticism or threats.
➤ Include them in decision-making.
➤ Help them include facts as well as feelings in their decision-making.
➤ Start conversations in a friendly manner.
➤ Have a system for resolving problems and conflicts.
➤ Be friendly.
➤ Do not ignore them.
➤ Provide opportunities to use their people skills.

| PUSHER ||
Communication Strengths	Possible Communication Weaknesses
Fast moving. Will keep a group aimed in the right direction. Sees new ideas and can get things done fast.	Tends to be forceful by telling people what to do. May become impatient with lots of detail and questions. Can override other peoples' ideas and feelings. May appear unfriendly and uncaring. Their motto is, "Just do it my way."

Pusher Communication Strategies

➤ Focus on the need for quick results.
➤ Avoid arguing or telling them they are wrong.
➤ Provide choices or options instead of telling them what to do.
➤ Do detailed research for them.
➤ Help them to consider people's feelings as well as become more patient and supportive.

Social Skill Builder 3:
Apply Emotional Intelligence to Diversity

Diversity competence has become a well-recognized need in today's working environment. Typically, diversity skills training focuses on different population groups as well as overcoming prejudice and stereotyping. Applying emotional intelligence skills to diversity is based on three assumptions:

➤ It is important to have emotionally intelligent communications tools that work well in most situations even when one is unsure about a person's background.

➤ You can never learn enough about different religions, customs, preferences, and needs to address the variety of associates and customers that you interact with daily.

➤ In certain situations, such as emergencies, it is important to quickly determine relevant information regarding a person's background and make suitable accommodations.

Obstacles to Cross-Cultural Communications

In addition to individual style differences, there are three barriers to effective cross-cultural communications:

1. One's world view or perspective

2. Cultural practices

3. Customs that influence emotional expression

1 One's world view or perspective is influenced by personal history such as age, gender, religion, geographical origins, family, personal experiences and traumas such as exposure to violence and prejudice.

Example: Abdi is an architect from Tunisia who works for an American firm with associates from many countries including India, Pakistan and Australia. Howard, an American associate recognizes that Abdi focuses exclusively on work and doesn't understand the concept of "lighten up." Their project team was working on a particularly time-consuming and important project. When Howard told Abdi that they would not be able to meet the client's deadline, Abdi said, "In my country, this would not be acceptable. We made a commitment. We will work harder!"

Describe the factors that influence your world view:

_____

_____

_____

_____

_____

Select someone who is quite different from you. Ask this person to describe the factors that affect his or her world view:

_____

_____

_____

_____

_____

2

Cultural practices govern behaviors such as politeness, respect, modesty, honesty and conflict. For example, in the United States, both men and women greet each other with a handshake and/or embrace. Others, such as Muslims or Orthodox Jews, consider male to female physical contact, other than family, inappropriate. In those instances, a verbal greeting and smile is appropriate.

Promptness is a cultural practice that may vary from culture to culture. For example, Wolfgang's parents were first-generation German Americans. He said, "While my home life had some serious freedom, I was always expected to be prompt, or notify my parents if there was cause to be off schedule. I never got away with being discourteous to elders, or for that matter my peers."

Based on your personal background, describe your cultural practices related to politeness and respect.

_____

_____

_____

_____

Based on your personal background, describe your cultural practices related to timeliness.

_____

_____

_____

_____

Select and observe someone who is quite different from your age, ethnicity, or religion and describe how this person treats others.

_____

_____

_____

_____

3 Customs influence emotional expression such as hiding feelings compared to unfettered demonstrations of joy, anger or sorrow. Cultural mores govern the extent to which conversations can be intimate versus impersonal or strictly factual. In some cultures, grief might be expressed with crying, tearing clothing and screaming; while in other cultures it is expected that people will be silently stoic.

Example: Most Southeast Asians are Buddhist, therefore, they believe that after people die, their family member will be reborn as another family member. Bounthanh explained that during the war in Laos, her parents experienced the deaths of two children. Although her parents cried publicly, their worldview was very positive about death. Because they are Buddhists, they kept the children close to their hearts by offering the deceased children's favorite foods or belongings via the Buddhist monk's chanting ceremony.

How does your family communicate or behave when someone is injured, becomes ill or dies?

_____

_____

_____

_____

_____

What have you observed about how people from other cultures act in similar circumstances?

_____

_____

_____

_____

_____

Overcome Cross-Cultural Misunderstandings

ALL x 2 = Ask & Answer + Look & Listen + Learn & Lift

Ask: If you're unsure about what a person says and more significantly what he or she means, ask questions. If you become frustrated or angry, it is best to stop and say…

"I'm not exactly sure what you just said. I do want to understand you. Would you kindly say it again more slowly so that my listening can adjust. Or, perhaps you can explain this to me in another way."

Sometimes a little humor can be helpful… "My ears have an accent, not you. Please be patient with me."

Answer: When someone asks you for clarification, don't laugh, become irate or defensive because he or she doesn't understand you. Explain what you mean by using simpler words and slowing down your speech. Imagine how difficult it would be to learn English when your original language is Hindi.

Beware the "rolling eyes" look of frustration or the sound of annoyance in your voice. Facial expressions and your tone of voice may be more important than the words you use with those from other cultures. A smile and gentle voice contribute to positive two-way communications.

Look: Observe how groups interact. Pause and watch whether individuals greet with a handshake, kisses on both cheeks, a bow, pat on the arm, smile or direct eye contact. Men in America generally greet each other with a handshake and energetic back pounding. In European countries, men may greet with hugs and kisses which might be viewed suspiciously by Americans.

Those from different backgrounds use varying degrees of formality. A man from India opens his memos formally and properly with "Dear Susan" rather than "Hi, hey, whazzup," or no greeting at all. He ends memos with a standard letter salutation such as "Sincerely Yours." Adjusting your style to his shows respect and increases the mutual trust in your communications—both oral and written.

Typically, Americans place a high value on direct eye contact and become wary when a business associate or candidate for employment avoids eye contact. In the American and mainstream European cultures, children are told to look parents in the eye when being chastised. In Hispanic society, children are taught to lower their gaze when being chastised. In the Hispanic context, eye contact is viewed as a challenge to the authority figure. Therefore, do not assume that a person is being disrespectful or lying if he or she does not make direct eye contact with you.

Interpret the Meaning of Expressions

"Most emotion researchers today agree that there are a limited number of basic emotions that all humans, in every culture, experience," according to Don and Sandy Hockenbury in their book, *Psychology* (pages 353 +).

The similarity of facial expressions across cultures is limited to basic emotions that seem to be "hard-wired" in our brains. The emotions of fear, disgust, surprise, happiness, anger and sadness are most often cited by researchers. There are some differences between men and women and among different cultures. Look for the subtle differences and do not make assumptions.

While women and men tend to be quite similar, in general, women tend to be more expressive. Men can more easily mask or cover their emotions. Therefore, men may present a smile that could be masking anger or fear. If you sense a disconnection between a man's smile and his words, listen, observe and ask for clarification.

In certain cultural contexts, the emotions of shame or embarrassment are significant. Among most Americans, these emotions are either nonexistent or minimal. As reported by Hockenburg and Hockenburg in one study involving Japanese people, shame rated much higher than anger. The cultural anthropologist Ruth Benedict describes shame as a violation of cultural or social values.

When communicating with people from a cultural context where the concept of "shame" is important, be sure to show respect such as for Buddhist monks, preachers, "elders" and those with highly-regarded professions: teachers, doctors as well as managers with titles. In order to "save face," Asians avoid shaming the individual in front of others with criticism, humiliation, ridicule, correction or isolation. In addition, Asians value family unity with harmony and integrity. Women who are divorced and/or disowned by their spouse are considered shameful.

Bounthanh who is from Laos explains that in the Southeast Asian villages, people know each other well. They are casual in addressing each other by first name basis with a title, such as aunty, uncle, brother, and/or sister. However, in front of outsiders, they are very humble and not too assertive. They never want to embarrass others.

Listen: Everyone has an accent from someplace. Americans from Long Island in New York State use different pronunciations for words like chocolate, oil and oranges than natives of southern Ohio. Grammar usage, pronunciation, speed and word choices may vary among English speakers from Pakistan, Great Britain, Australia, and the United States.

With patience and good will, the human ear has a remarkable ability to adjust. An Imam from Iraq speaks extremely fast with a distinctive accent. Over time, it seemed that his English improved. In reality, the listener's hearing simply adjusted as a result of attentive listening and repeated interaction.

Learn: The more you know about different world views, customs, expressions and etiquette, the easier it will be to work and live side by side. There are many ways to learn including via the media, interfaith groups, resources on different cultures, movies about the lives and values of various populations.

When time and familiarity permit, a wonderful way to learn is to encourage interaction, such as, "I'd appreciate knowing more about your country and your customs. How do people from your culture handle inter-personal communications regarding disagreement, anger or correction?"

Lift: Raise your own and others' comfort levels as you interact by smiling, using words from their language as well as carefully selected humor. According to Goleman in his book *Social Intelligence* (page 44), "…genuine smiles of spontaneous pleasure or amusement…are most likely to evoke one in return."

Learn a few words of various languages to facilitate connections. Search for "hello in other languages" on the Internet or just ask for the proper words and their pronunciation. Sometimes names can be difficult to pronounce; once again, ask for help and practice.

Welcome

Marhaban (Arabic), *Aloha mai* (Hawaiian), *Baruch haba* (Hebrew), *Benvenuto* (Italian), *Soo dowatha* (Somali), *Bienvenidos* (Spanish)

Goodbye

Salaam (Arabic), *Au revoir* (French), *Shalom* (Hebrew), *Namaste* (Hindi), *Ciao* (Italian), *Sayonara* (Japanese), *Nabad gelyo* (Somali), *Adios* (Spanish), *Sizobanana* (Zulu)

What forms of greeting and good bye are used by your family, friends and associates? _____

_____

What words in other languages and cultures have you learned?

_____

Humor and jokes are natural and easy among people from the same culture because they share common experiences, customs and expressions. Cross-cultural humor can be a delicate matter. Following are guidelines for consideration:

> ➤ Be sure that the words you use will be understood by your listeners. Slang such as "that's cool," may not make sense to people who haven't grown up in America.

> ➤ Avoid humor that shows disdain for a group of people, such as those with disabilities.

> ➤ Test your jokes in advance with friends and associates from different backgrounds. If your company has a diversity council, this might be a wonderful group to engage in a discussion about humor at work.

> ➤ If you are not sure, don't say it. Jokes related to sexuality and religion may be risky.

> ➤ Do find natural humor in the world around you and in true situations.

> ➤ Observe what makes people laugh in your work environment.

Plan a strategy for your response when you are at the receiving end of offensive humor. Consider the outcome that you are trying to achieve such as keeping a positive relationship, stopping the behavior, educating the person, improving service to customers.

Generally, it is better to have a private conversation when you (or others) have been embarrassed or offended by someone's attempt at humor. Following are emotionally intelligent discussion starters:

> ➤ I am very uncomfortable when we make fun of…because he/ she…has an accent, makes grammatical mistakes, wears distinctive clothing, etc. If I don't say anything, it may seem that I think this type of humor is acceptable conversation.

> ➤ I'm not sure that you are aware of how or why that comment or joke is hurtful to people.

> ➤ I think I didn't "get it." Would you please explain what makes that funny?

Apply ALL x 2

<hr>

CASE STUDY: The Newspaper

Takilo, a newspaper editor from Somalia is challenged by ever-present time deadlines. He is very polite, complimentary and peppers his conversation with frequent "thank you's."

Janine has difficulty understanding him on the phone due to his accent, speed and background noise. Both Janine and Takilo are excellent writers. In person, both Takilo and Janine smile warmly and shake hands when they meet. Occasionally, there have been misunderstandings regarding timelines, financial arrangements and specifications regarding length of articles.

Develop an ALL script that Janine can use to improve clarity and efficiency.

ALL x 2 = Ask & Answer + Look & Listen + Learn & Lift

Ask _____

Answer _____

Look _____

Listen _____

Learn _____

Lift _____

CASE STUDY: Customers with Disabilities

Thomas and Sarah work for a restaurant that is trying to teach associates how to serve customers properly. They used the following personal experience to illustrate the importance of understanding how to serve those with disabilities.

During a business luncheon, the server who took Thomas' order asked him what Sarah wanted. Thomas told the server to ask Sarah directly. The server said, "I can't tell where she is looking." (Sarah had strabismus-crossed eyes.) Of course, Sarah was offended and embarrassed. She vowed never to return to that restaurant.

Apply the ALL script to training that the restaurant can use to help their employees serve those with disabilities.

ALL x 2 = Ask & Answer + Look & Listen + Learn & Lift

Ask _____

Answer _____

Look _____

Listen _____

Learn _____

Lift _____

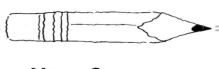

YOUR SITUATION

Are you working with someone from another generation, culture, country, different part of your country? Describe his or her background:

_____

Describe at least one cross-cultural communication challenge that you would like to improve in the future:

_____

Review the previous section and prepare an ALL script for the next time you have cross-cultural challenges with this person. Remember, this script can be used in writing, when talking on the phone or in person as well as during meetings.

ALL x 2 = Ask & Answer + Look & Listen + Learn & Lift

Ask   _____

Answer _____

Look   _____

Listen _____

Learn   _____

Lift   _____

After you "try out" your ALL script, return to this section and assess your interaction.

Did I approach _____ with patience and good will?   ❏ Yes   ❏ No

Did _____ react positively when I used the ALL script?   ❏ Yes   ❏ No

Have our interactions improved as a result?   ❏ Yes   ❏ No

What did I learn from this "try out?"   _____

_____

What will I re-use next time?   _____

_____

What will I do differently?   _____

_____

Strategy 2: Emotional Control

Emotionally intelligent people are able to adapt their emotional expression to the situations in which they find themselves. They do not over-control or stifle their natural feelings. Neither do they have emotional outbursts of negative feelings.

Author Daniel Goleman uses the idea of emotional hijacking when people are so overwhelmed by their feelings that they act without concern for their own or others' safety. They are out of control and do not think about what they are doing. Some people even say they have no memory of what happened after they were hijacked by their instincts and emotions. Strong emotions could include fear, anger, as well as the positive emotions of love and compassion.

In a busy metropolitan airport, a traveler angrily throws his briefcase into a plate glass window. Within moments, airport security guards wrestle him to the ground, handcuff him, and lead him away. Why did the man have such an angry explosion? The plane he was waiting to board was cancelled.

Anger stole away this person's good sense. What did this outburst of emotion accomplish for the traveler? What could he have done differently?

When peoples' angry emotions take over their logic, it is very difficult to communicate effectively. From time to time, everyone has to deal with a person who loses control. Sometimes it is an associate, a supervisor, a customer, or oneself. Angry feelings are like a thief. They steal away the part of your brain that keeps you from saying things you regret later. Angry feelings sometimes become so intense that people become verbally abusive or physically violent.

The benefits of using emotional control are that you will be able to:

➤ Select better responses to challenging people and situations

➤ Become more calm and peaceful when you have to deal with stress

➤ Help others deal with their angry feelings

➤ Avoid physical or verbal violence

The challenges to controlling emotions are:

➤ One's own anger

➤ Others' anger directed at you

➤ Stress and negativity

➤ Poor role models

Two Phases of Emotional Control

Phase 1: Before you can respond to others' anger, it is essential to manage your own overwhelming feelings.

Phase 2: Prepare yourself for responding appropriately to others when they become angry, frustrating, and irritating toward you.

Emotional Controller 1: Keep Your Brain Engaged

Prepare yourself by understanding what causes you to become angry. Anger has many causes.

What causes you to lose emotional control?

- ❑ When you feel that you have no choices or options
- ❑ When you are in physical or emotional danger
- ❑ When you are treated unfairly
- ❑ When you are disappointed with yourself for making a mistake
- ❑ When something or someone gets in the way of what you want to do
- ❑ When you feel someone has violated your values such as by lying to you
- ❑ Other:

Three Steps to Become Calm

These critical steps take only a few seconds. They can make the difference between losing control and gaining it. These steps will help you to calm down.

1. Slow down your breathing rate and speak softly. Take a breath and relax.

2. Become aware of your feelings. Are you embarrassed, offended, frightened, or confused? Recall that certain situations cause you to lose control. For example, you may become frustrated when you are rushing to reach a deadline.

3. Understand the true cause of your reactions. Are you upset because you have been unjustly accused of doing something?

Emotional Controller 2:
Prepare a Script to Handle Angry People

Prepare a script to deal with someone who is using you as the target for his/her anger. A script is a plan of action. If you have a plan, it will be easier for you to keep control of your own emotions. Once you feel calm, use the UART script. The UART (pronounced *wart*) system is a method for dealing with angry people who are like warts. The angry person and a wart can be hard to get rid of—irritating and painful.

Understand. Listen carefully and calmly, and get the angry person to talk about his or her feelings. Restate in your words what you believe the angry person is trying to say. For example, "Mrs. Johnson, you are upset because you called us three times and no one returned your call. Is that right?"

Apologize. Most angry people feel they have been treated unfairly. They will feel less angry when they receive a sincere apology. Do not blame others by saying things like "Those people in shipping never answer their telephones." It would be better to say, "Mrs. Johnson, I apologize for the wasted time. You should not have had to call three times."

Resolve the Problem. Do what you can to solve the problem. If you cannot do so immediately, explain what you can do and when it will be done. Give Mrs. Johnson your telephone number so she can call you back if there are any further problems. Most of the time, peoples' anger will have decreased by this point in the conversation. In the event they are still angry and you are beginning to feel that your emotions are out-of-control, take the next step.

Take a Break. If you feel one or more of the following is happening, it is time to take a break.

> ➤ Emotions are becoming dangerous.

> ➤ You are about to say something you'll regret later.

> ➤ The other person is yelling and red in the face.

> ➤ You or the other person is out of emotional control.

> ➤ Whatever you say or do makes no difference.

A break can be anywhere from five minutes to as long as 24 hours. You might say this, "I need a few minutes to check out some information. I'd like to give us both a few minutes to think this over. Can we talk again in 15 minutes?"

Avoid using accusative language, such as, "You are too upset." A better option is "I or we are too upset to solve problems now." The second phrasing is less likely to cause defensiveness. The key is to make certain that you establish a later time to resolve the problem when all parties have a chance to become calm.

PRACTICE THE **UART** METHOD

Think of a situation at work when someone became angry with you. Use the UART method to write out an action plan for dealing with this angry person. Describe how you would:

Understand

_____

_____

_____

Apologize

_____

_____

_____

Resolve the Problem

_____

_____

_____

Take a Break

_____

_____

_____

Emotional Controller 3: Confront Negators

Emotionally intelligent people confront negative people when they cannot be avoided. Negators (negative people) tend to get worse rather than better if others tolerate their behavior. If you confront the negative people in your life in a positive and objective manner, you help them see how their behavior affects others and limits their own success. One way to make this confrontation effective is to prepare a script. This script should include an objective description of the person's behavior and an honest explanation of how that behavior makes you feel.

Imagine that Jeremy is a negator and a member of your project team. He constantly complains about what won't work. He finds things wrong with every suggestion for improvement. Generally, he is pretty unhappy with work and shares his outlook with everyone.

Here is a possible script for confronting Jeremy:

Give yourself a positive message.

Script: "I can talk to Jeremy about his negativity and its impact on me."

Objectively describe Jeremy's actions.

Script: "When we try to come up with a solution, you say why it won't work."

Describe how his negativity affects you.

Script: "I feel frustrated because we don't spend enough time on how to make our projects work. Instead we spend our time analyzing what's wrong with a particular solution."

Be prepared to say what you will do if the negative person's actions continue.

Script: "If you continue to do this, I will let you know my reactions. And, we may have to work out the problems without your input."

Follow through on your promise.

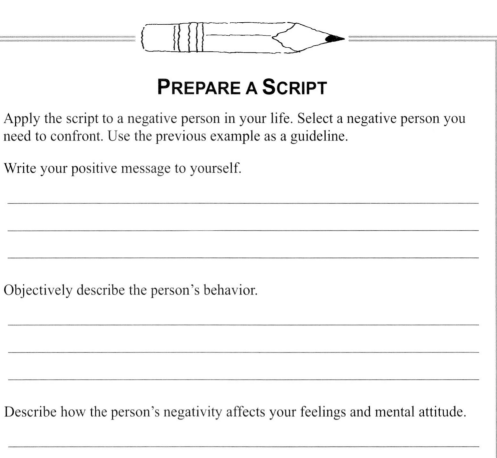

PREPARE A SCRIPT

Apply the script to a negative person in your life. Select a negative person you need to confront. Use the previous example as a guideline.

Write your positive message to yourself.

_____

_____

_____

Objectively describe the person's behavior.

_____

_____

_____

Describe how the person's negativity affects your feelings and mental attitude.

_____

_____

_____

State what you will do if the behavior continues.

_____

_____

_____

Follow through.

_____

_____

_____

Emotional Controller 4: Build Up Your Energy

When stress continues for a long period of time, the body may burn out physically, mentally, and emotionally. Chronic stress interferes with concentration and the logical brain. It becomes increasingly more difficult to deal with angry associates, frustrated clients, or a demanding supervisor. When you are physically and emotionally healthy, you can deal with a threat or a crisis.

Research indicates that stress contributes to 80% of major illness, is responsible for 75% to 90% of doctor's visits and costs businesses as much as $300 billion a year. Repeated stress results in a weaker immune system. People with weaker immune systems are unable to heal and fight off diseases as well as those with stronger immune systems. The more stressors you have in your life at one time, the greater the chance that you will become ill.

Sources of Stress

> ➤ Major life events such as the death of a loved one, getting married, having a baby, buying a house, losing a job, or getting a divorce.

> ➤ Continuous and unpredictable change, poor relationship with one's supervisor, unrealistic workload, or a negative work environment.

> ➤ Daily hassles such as misplacing or losing things, being in heavy traffic, worrying about your job security, finances or having too many things to do.

> ➤ Poor relationships at work with associates, management, or customers.

MANAGING YOUR STRESS

Stress can't be stopped, but it can be interrupted or managed. Emotionally intelligent people use the following strategies to help them manage stress. Check the strategies that you believe will be helpful for you to increase.

❏ Take care of your physical needs through exercise, rest, and nutrition.

❏ Get enough sleep.

❏ Build positive relationships with family and friends.

❏ Do something you enjoy every day.

❏ Increase your satisfaction level at work, at home, and during your leisure time.

❏ Use positive messages to yourself and others by finding new ways to perceive changes.

❏ Have periods of relaxation or enjoyment to break up the periods of stress during the day or week. These can vary from a brief break every hour to a two-week or longer vacation.

❏ Take a full 24-hour break from work once a week.

❏ Combine a lunch break with a stress break. Avoid thinking about or doing work during this time. If you have time before or after you eat lunch, take a walk, talk to friends, read a book, or stretch.

❏ Meet your spiritual needs through prayer, involvement in your spiritual community, and meditation.

❏ Take a few minutes to imagine a restful, calming place such as the beach or a rambling brook.

KNOW WHEN TO ASK FOR HELP

Consider getting help from a qualified professional if you feel you need it. If you answer "Yes" to four or more of the following questions, consider seeing a family physician, counselor, or spiritual leader:

	Yes	No
Do you find yourself becoming angry or irritated with others four or more times per day?	❑	❑
During the last year, have you become apathetic (given up) about most things at work and in your personal life?	❑	❑
Do you feel down and unhappy most of the time?	❑	❑
Do you have trouble concentrating at work?	❑	❑
Do you feel most people don't want to talk to you?	❑	❑
Do you feel tired most of the time?	❑	❑
Do you have trouble sleeping through the night?	❑	❑
Do you have trouble with food? Eat too much, not enough, or the wrong foods?	❑	❑
Do you worry about things most of the time?	❑	❑
Do you feel lonely most of the time?	❑	❑

Control Work Responsibilities

How often do you find you just cannot take on another responsibility? Do you have difficulty saying "no"? If you take on more and more work responsibilities without managing your workload, you may find your work becoming less rewarding and enjoyable. Over time, it becomes difficult to stay positive and optimistic. Learn how to use appropriate assertiveness. Learn how to break up a project into manageable parts.

Prepare yourself to speak to your supervisor or co-workers by using the following approach:

1. Describe your work responsibilities that are overwhelming you.

2. Explain how you and your work are affected.

3. Provide options.

4. Make a commitment.

Sample Script 1

"I know we all have tight deadlines. Right now I am so overwhelmed with the quantity of work on my desk that the quality is beginning to suffer. Can you help me prioritize all my projects? If it's okay, I will try to find shortcuts. It is my goal to do everything properly and on time."

Sample Script 2

"We're all struggling with the changes in our computer system. Let's see if we can break up this project into more manageable parts. We each have special strengths; perhaps we can divide up the work a little differently. Some of us may be better at using the new software program. Let's also figure out how we can help each other. I will help by training our team."

CREATE YOUR SCRIPT

Based on the examples, write your own script for talking to another person about how to manage your workload.

Describe the work responsibilities that are overwhelming you:

_____

_____

_____

Explain how you and your work are affected:

_____

_____

_____

Provide options:

_____

_____

_____

Ask for help:

_____

_____

_____

State your commitment:

_____

_____

_____

The Big Four Energizers

Chronic stress at home and work are problems in addition to the stressors already described. Chronic stress has a greater negative impact than periodic stress because it impairs one's immune system. There is a causal relationship between the incidence of chronic stress and physical and mental illness. Four energizers can break up chronic stress by creating good-feeling chemicals in your brain. Beta-endorphins give you a natural high feeling and strengthen your immune system.

Energizer 1: Exercise

Smart exercise is physical activity that raises your heart and breathing rate and results in sweating. Most health experts suggest 20 to 40 minutes a day 3 to 5 times a week. However, even smaller amounts help. Check with your doctor about the type of exercise best for you. This is especially important with increasing age. An excellent exercise program could be as simple as taking a brisk half-hour walk five times a week.

Energizer 2: Laughter

Having a good sense of humor about yourself and others is important. Don't laugh at the expense of others, but laugh with them about everyday events. Break up your day with periods of laughter and joy. Have you ever seen a funny movie or heard a funny story and laughed so hard your belly shook and you cried? Belly laughing increases heart rate, breathing rate, and forms endorphins in your brain.

Energizer 3: Caring

Caring is positive emotional contact with someone. Loving someone or feeling that another cares for you causes feel-good chemicals to form in your brain. Positive emotional contact includes giving and receiving support, giving and receiving encouragement, and helping others. Both the receiver and the giver receive benefits. Having a loved pet also makes people feel good because of the caring relationship.

Energizer 4: Hot Peppers

One of the ingredients of hot peppers is capsaicin. When digested there is an increase in the level of beta-endorphins in the brain which causes us to feel good and fight off illness. However, do not eat hot peppers if they upset your digestive system.

What energizers are you using now to help manage your stress?

_____

What energizers would you like to add to your life?

_____

Strategy 3: Flexibility

During the course of any business day, all kinds of changes can happen. A new supervisor from another country or company can raise the anxiety level. An emergency telephone call, a computer breakdown, or a family illness can cause delays and frustration. What changes happened yesterday that required you to quickly adapt?

The benefits of being more flexible are that you will:

> ➤ Find the best opportunities in your life

> ➤ Use your energy productively when changes occur

> ➤ Stay calm and relaxed during moments of unexpected change

> ➤ Use your emotional intelligence as well as logic to solve problems during transitions

> ➤ Build on your strengths and past successes

> ➤ Help others handle their stressful days

The challenges to becoming more flexible are:

> ➤ Wasting energy

> ➤ Resisting change

> ➤ Staying stuck

Flexibility Enhancer 1: Use Your Energy Wisely

Flexibility increases when people feel they have control over their lives and can make choices. Flexible people are willing to try new ideas.

Distinguish between those things that you cannot change and those that you can change. Following is a partial list of examples. The column on the left includes things that individuals usually cannot change by themselves. The center column lists things that individuals may change through problem solving with others. The column on the right lists things that an individual usually can change. Check the items in each column that apply to you and add your own examples in the blank spaces.

Things I cannot change	Things that may be changed with others	Things I can change
➤ The weather ➤ The economy ➤ The laws, rules, and regulations that affect business ➤ The way others behave	➤ How others talk to me ➤ Priorities and goals for our department ➤ How my team members help each other ➤ My work schedule	➤ My attitude and education ➤ The way I plan my day ➤ How I take care of myself (exercise, nutrition, and rest) ➤ How I communicate with others ➤ What gets me upset
Add more:	Add more:	Add more:

PUT YOUR ENERGY WHERE IT COUNTS

If you find yourself worrying and complaining about things you cannot change, then you will have less time and energy to use creative problem solving for things that really can make a difference. Invest your energy in more of the items in the center and right columns. Put less of your energy into items in the left column.

What are two things that you cannot change?

_____

_____

What are two things that you should discuss with others that may be changed?

_____

_____

What do you believe are two things that you can change?

_____

_____

Flexibility Enhancer 2: Change Yourself

Rigid and unbending people become anxious, angry, and resist change. They may say, "If it ain't broke, don't fix it. It's OK to make changes over in that other department, but not in mine." By focusing on the negative aspects of a change, they reduce their ability to think clearly and see options. They may act in ways that are not helpful for themselves and others. They see little relationship between their actions and what happens in their lives.

HOW DO YOU REACT TO CHANGE?

On the scale below, circle the number that is nearest to the way you handle change.

10 = You are flexible and adaptable most of the time

1 = You are rigid and unbending most of the time

Flexible   10   9   8   7   6   5   4   3   2   1   **Rigid**

Ask one or more trusted friends to rate you also. Ask them to give you examples of how they think you adapt to change. After comparing your rating to theirs, what did you learn about yourself?

Flexibility Enhancer 3: Focus on Positives

Use success thinking to recall when you skillfully handled change in another time and place. Think of examples of your past successes in dealing with change and being flexible. What did you learn from those experiences that will be helpful to you now and that you might share with others?

Build on Strengths

When you are doing something that involves a strength, you can become deeply lost in your work and lose track of time. Some people have a natural ability to learn new computer programs; some have a natural ability to teach others.

A strength is something that:

> ➤ You do well and easily

> ➤ Brings great satisfaction and pleasure

> ➤ You learn easily

> ➤ Helps you to feel energized and satisfied when it is a major part of your work

> ➤ May be difficult to recognize

Identify Your Own Strengths

You may want to review the four communication styles (Social Skill Builder 2 in this part of the book) to identify some of your strengths. Ask a trusted friend to give you feedback.

What are three of your most important strengths?

_____

_____

_____

Flexibility Enhancer 4: Explore Options to Solve Problems

Flexible people use creativity to find different ways to solve problems. Rigid unbending people may see change as negative and something to be resisted. Resistant thinking stops people from moving forward and finding positive opportunities in change.

Ten Approaches for New Solutions

1. Use reverse thinking. See change as a creative opportunity rather than a stifling problem.

2. Find out how other people cope with a similar problem.

3. Make small improvements in things you are doing now. If you already have a habit of daily planning at work, consider how you can apply your planning strategy to your personal life.

4. Learn more about the transitions occurring in your business or company. Help yourself and others expand personal skills to adapt positively.

5. Work cooperatively. When people from diverse backgrounds work together to solve a problem, everyone is more likely to be satisfied and support the group solution. When groups agree on common goals, everyone becomes more involved.

6. Keep an open mind. While you are looking for options, hear new ideas and keep an open heart. Do not block out feelings, ideas, or thinking.

7. Take a break. Put your problem on the shelf and come back to it later. When you return, you may see new solutions that were not obvious when you were tired and discouraged.

8. Develop a flexible plan. Use the following questions to develop a flexible plan:
   What will we do differently if circumstances change?
   What changes do we anticipate for the future and how can we prepare ourselves?
   What options do I have personally?
   What is the worst or best thing that could happen?
   If the worst happens, what alternatives do I or we have?
   What can I do personally to help myself stay flexible?

9. Add fun to change. Find new and positive ways to welcome change. Hold a contest for the most humorous predictions.

10. Remember that the worst events sometimes produce the best outcomes. Have you or your friends lost a job and then discovered that the change resulted in a much better career? Have you survived a divorce and discovered a "new you"? Did you add a new person to your life who was even better than the one who caused your sorrows?

"Be Smart" Summary

An Action Plan for Using "Be Smart" People Strategies

Review the Be Smart Strategies for improving interpersonal relationships. Fill in action steps you will take to become smarter as you interact with others.

Strategy 1: Social skills action options include:

➤ Listening intently and compassionately

➤ Personalizing communications to the unique needs of each person

➤ Applying emotional intelligence to cross-cultural communications

The steps I plan to take to improve my social skills are:

_____

_____

_____

_____

Strategy 2: Flexibility includes:

➤ Putting your energy into things you can change

➤ Improving yourself

➤ Building on your strengths

➤ Finding options to solve problems

The steps I plan to take to adapt to change are:

_____

_____

_____

_____

Strategy 3: Controlling one's emotions includes the following action options:

➤ Becoming calm

➤ Using a prepared script to handle anger

➤ Giving feedback to negative people

➤ Developing coping skills for managing stress

The steps I plan to take to control my emotions are:

_____

_____

_____

_____

P A R T 3

"Work Smart" Strategies

Six Strategies for Smart Organizations

> *The smart organization is more than just a workplace. It is a business community that is alive, exciting, and adaptable."*
>
> *—Executive EQ* **by Robert K. Cooper and Ayman Sawa**

The benefits of having a smart business community are that people will:

- ➤ Be enthusiastic and excited by their work

- ➤ Get involved because they want to be involved

- ➤ Be willing to take on big challenges

- ➤ Act upbeat and positive

- ➤ Encourage others

- ➤ Work hard on their own

- ➤ Show customers that they—the customers—really matter

In the book, *Executive EQ*, the authors describe the people who work in smart organizations as those who have "the inner fire required to build great companies and compete for the future."

To make an organization more than "just a workplace," build a community in which emotionally plus intellectually smart people can thrive by using six strategies:

1. Practice organizational self-awareness via assessment.

2. Develop social skills with training and application.

3. Foster optimism.

4. Encourage flexibility and problem solving.

5. Model and encourage emotional control.

6. Support teamwork.

Strategy 1: Practice Organizational Self-Awareness

Smart organizations continuously assess what they are doing to foster enthusiasm, passion, and emotional intelligence at work. Use self-assessments, surveys, and other data-gathering tools to stay in tune with your organization and people with whom you work. Invite others to participate with you in this self-awareness exercise.

Compare the business practices in your organization to those in the following list. Assess whether you engage in these practices well or could do better. Refer to explanations of the Six Strategies for Smart Organizations in this Part.

Smart Business Practices	Strategies for Smart Organizations
Periodically assess levels of emotional intelligence in our workplace. ❑ We do well ❑ We could do better	Practice Self-Assessment: Strategy 1
Provide training on the basic job skills PLUS training on effective communi-cations and emotional control. ❑ We do well ❑ We could do better	Develop Social Skills: Strategy 2
Help everyone understand how his or her work connects to our mission. ❑ We do well ❑ We could do better	Foster Optimism and Passion: Strategy 3
Let people see that you are striving to have a better future for customers as well as employees. ❑ We do well ❑ We could do better	Foster Optimism and Passion: Strategy 4
Give people the opportunity to learn how anticipated future changes affect their current work. ❑ We do well ❑ We could do better	Encourage Flexibility and Problem Solving: Strategy 5
Have guidelines and practices that ensure everyone will be treated with respect. ❑ We do well ❑ We could do better	Model and Encourage Emotional Control: Strategy 5
Use team guidelines to ensure open communications and protect people from personal attacks when discussing difficult issues. ❑ We do well ❑ We could do better	Support Teamwork: Strategy 6
Ensure that associates from diverse backgrounds participate in team decisions. ❑ We do well ❑ We could do better	Support Teamwork: Strategy 6
Have fun. ❑ We do well ❑ We could do better	Support Teamwork: Strategy 6

CREATING A SMART ORGANIZATION

What are the two most important smart organizational practices that you are doing well?

_____

_____

_____

_____

What are the two most important smart practices that you could do better?

_____

_____

_____

_____

The following descriptions of work smart strategies will help you learn how to build on your existing smart business practices and make improvements.

Strategy 2: Develop Social Skills

Social skills are considered as important, if not more important, than technical job-related skills. Social skills are based on the ability to communicate and relate well with others. Effective business communities provide continuous training and development on technical skills *plus* social skills. What's the difference between the two?

Comparison of Social Skills to Technical Skills

Assume that you wish to purchase a laptop computer for the first time. You have always used desktop models and don't know anything about laptops. You research your options with two stores, Store A and Store B.

Store A: Chris asks what you're looking for. He shows you several laptops. He tells you about the features and benefits of each laptop in great detail. It is obvious that Chris is extremely knowledgeable about computers and the products that his company offers. You become increasingly confused while Chris is talking, but he never notices. You are reluctant to ask questions because you feel stupid. He gives you the prices and asks how you would like to pay for the computer. You are feeling overwhelmed with the choices and unsure of what you want or need. When you start to explain your confusion, Chris sounds frustrated and loses interest in helping you.

Store B: Sandy asks what you're looking for. She asks if you have had any experience with a laptop or desktop computer. She also asks how you intend to use a laptop. As you answer the questions, Sandy listens intently and restates in her own words what she believes your needs are. She is careful to use words you understand when she explains the features and benefits of each option. You ask a number of questions and Sandy responds clearly and patiently. You feel she really wants to help you make the best selection.

COMPARING SKILLS

Which of the following positive social skills did Chris, in Store A, use effectively?

- ❏ Understanding and expressing himself effectively.
- ❏ Listening carefully to you.
- ❏ Helping you express your feelings.
- ❏ Adapting his communication style to your needs.

Which of the following social skills did Sandy, in Store B, use effectively?

- ❏ Understanding and expressing herself effectively.
- ❏ Listening carefully to you.
- ❏ Helping you express your feelings.
- ❏ Adapting her communication style to your needs.

	A	B
At which store do you believe the company has provided effective social skills training?	❏	❏
Which sales person do you prefer?	❏	❏

Why?

_____

_____

_____

Imagine that you are Chris's manager. What will be your biggest challenge in getting Chris to use social skills? The challenge is changing the communication habits that he has developed over his lifetime. The following skill builders will help learners like Chris develop and refine social skills.

Social Skills Builder 1:
Use "Emotions-On" Training

Actively involve the learner's senses (seeing, touching and feeling) in a lifelike experience. For Chris, a good technique would be to put him into a role-playing situation in which he plays the buyer. Help him to experience what it's like to purchase something that is not in his area of expertise.

Social Skills Builder 2:
Have a Positive Relationship with the Learner

Trainers who utilize feelings as well as facts and are open to new ideas are more likely to produce emotional changes than those who are critical, pushy, aggressive, and inflexible. A good coach or trainer would encourage Chris to express his reactions to the uninformed customer as well as help Chris to share his frustrations when he loses a potential buyer.

Social Skills Builder 3:
Connect Learning to Doing

Managers play an important role in helping trainees take new skills from the training situation to their work. Managers can give positive feedback when they see an employee trying out skills they learned during training. Observe the person for a period of time after training and ask these questions: What have you done differently as a result of the training? How has it helped you to increase your sales? How can I support you in your efforts to be more successful?

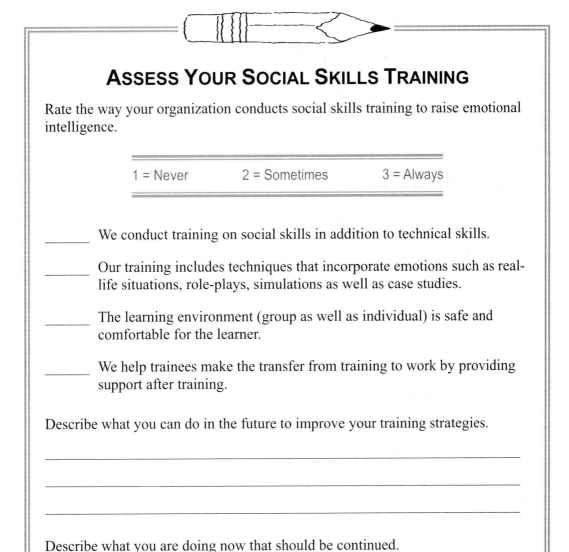

ASSESS YOUR SOCIAL SKILLS TRAINING

Rate the way your organization conducts social skills training to raise emotional intelligence.

| 1 = Never | 2 = Sometimes | 3 = Always |

_____ We conduct training on social skills in addition to technical skills.

_____ Our training includes techniques that incorporate emotions such as real-life situations, role-plays, simulations as well as case studies.

_____ The learning environment (group as well as individual) is safe and comfortable for the learner.

_____ We help trainees make the transfer from training to work by providing support after training.

Describe what you can do in the future to improve your training strategies.

_____

_____

_____

Describe what you are doing now that should be continued.

_____

_____

_____

Strategy 3: Foster Optimism

Optimism is a belief that the future can be better than the present. Optimists work steadily toward achieving a goal despite obstacles. Optimists also believe that what they do can have an impact on outcomes. Negativism and pessimism erode enthusiasm and hope.

Challenges that get in the way of fostering optimism:

> ➤ People do not feel the organization's future goals relate to them.

> ➤ The organization creates a negative environment.

> ➤ Individuals have little or no decision-making power or control over how or what they do.

In 2008, the U. S. military engaged roughly 40,000 returning soldiers in a standardized "Army Redeployment Survey" to determine why young officers were leaving in record numbers. The findings indicated that the young officers wanted to participate in helping choose their next assignments. The officers did not make a commitment to more years of service in order to gain additional control over their own futures.

Optimism Raiser 1: Connect the Present to the Future

Smart business communities help employees to see a connection between their work and the company's goals. A successful business community has a commitment to a future that will be better for employees as well as for customers. When people know they are working toward a goal for themselves and the company, they feel more positive about the future.

COMPARE TWO GOALS

Goal A: We want to treat our customers so well that they can't wait to come back.

Goal B: We want to treat our customers *and* employees so well that they can't wait to come back.

What is the difference between the two goal statements?

_____

_____

_____

_____

	A	**B**
Which goal would help you to feel more optimistic and involved?	❏	❏
Review your business goal. Is it more like goal A or goal B?	❏	❏

Establishing Organizational Goals

Discuss your goals for the future:

➤ With everyone

➤ Frequently

➤ When setting individual goals and priorities

➤ During all-staff meetings

➤ While you are training

➤ When giving feedback

➤ At performance review time

Use questions to stimulate feelings *plus* thinking about the company goal, such as:

➤ How do you think it feels (positive and negative) to be one of our customers?

➤ What experiences (positive and negative) do customers have when they come here?

➤ Why do customers use our products or services?

➤ What do you believe customers think our goal is?

➤ How does it feel (positive and negative) to be an employee?

➤ What experiences (positive and negative) do employees have who work here?

➤ Why do individuals work for this organization?

➤ What do you believe is our goal for employees?

➤ Do you feel respected and valued by your supervisor and associates?

Optimism Raiser 2:
Assess Level of Optimism versus Pessimism

This exercise is about understanding your organization's level of optimism compared to pessimism so that you can take positive steps in the right direction. Put an "X" on the line above the number that is nearest to the way you believe people feel about their work.

10 = People are optimistic most of the time

1 = People are pessimistic most of the time

Optimistic & positive	10	9	8	7	6	5	4	3	2	1	Pessimistic & negative

Ask your associates to use this scale to assess themselves and others. Ask them to give you examples of how they show their positive, optimistic outlook. After comparing your rating to theirs, what did you learn about your organization?

Assessing Pessimism

Find out what is lowering optimism and creating a negative outlook at your workplace by checking the statements that apply.

People have a hard time staying positive because they:

❑ Keep running into obstacles.

❑ Hear a lot of negativity and complaining.

❑ Believe their efforts are taken for granted.

❑ Are constantly criticized.

❑ Receive critical feedback to the exclusion of positive feedback.

❑ Are treated disrespectfully.

❑ Aren't supported by management.

❑ Experience frequent and unpredictable changes.

❑ Have too many things to do and not enough time to do a good job.

What is happening at your organization that tends to lower enthusiasm and optimism?

Assessing Optimism

Find out what is raising optimism and a positive outlook at your workplace by checking the statements that apply.

Positive beliefs about the future tend to increase for workers because they:

- ❑ Believe their leaders are positive and optimistic.

- ❑ Know that what they do makes a difference to their work or helps someone.

- ❑ Feel they are important.

- ❑ Believe that they have some control over how they do their work and how decisions are made.

- ❑ Have support from their managers and team of associates.

- ❑ Are accurately and honestly informed about what is happening with both the good and bad news.

What is happening at your organization that tends to raise enthusiasm and optimism?

Strategy 4: Encourage Flexibility and Problem Solving

Like people, organizations need to stretch in order to keep flexible. Flexible organizations adapt more readily to changing circumstances than those that become rigid from staying the same. Flexible organizations continuously look for ways to improve. Do you know of any businesses that died because they did not change quickly enough to adapt to changes?

Flexibility Skill Builder 1: Imagine the Future

Keep people flexible by stimulating their imaginations to feel what life will be like in the future. Ask these questions in discussions, meetings, conferences and retreats:

➤ What changes do you anticipate will affect the way we do our business? Encourage people to consider demographic, technological, medical, political, environmental, economic and other types of changes.

➤ What are we doing now that will still be successful in five or ten years? Encourage discussion about what you provide, how you deliver it and to whom.

Journey Backwards from the Future

In your imagination, get as close as you can to actually experiencing a future world in your organization. Visualize how your work place will be transformed in the future:

➤ How do you imagine the business will look and feel in five years? In ten years?

➤ What will the people be like who work in the future business? What skills and knowledge will they need?

➤ What do you think should be done now to prepare for anticipated changes individually and collectively?

➤ Where will you be working, for example, in an office, on the road, from your home or via some technology yet to be conceived?

➤ How can changes be turned into opportunities for a better future for customers and employees?

Study and Share Future Trends

Learn about trends so that you can create a bright future for your organization. In 1996, authors Faith Popcorn and Lys Marigold, predicted the Fantasy Adventure Trend in their book, Clicking. This trend is still visible today when you visit adult and children's theme parks, adventure retail stores, and new shopping malls. In the book, *The Learning Revolution*, authors Gordon Dryden and Dr. Jeannette Vos anticipate 16 major trends including these: instant communications; no economic borders; women in leadership plus the powers of the brain unleashed.

On March 24, 2008, *Time* magazine devoted an issue to 10 ideas that are changing the world such as the end of customer service, the need for geo-engineering to fix nature, living within our means, and employers requiring employees to take care of their health.

In the 2008 book, *Globality: Competing With Everyone From Everywhere For Everything*, the authors urge U.S. companies to "adapt, adopt and synthesize ideas from everyone and everywhere."

What trends do you know about that can help your organization make smart decisions? Changes in technology? Healthcare and medical research? Consumers' preferences and personal values? Where people come from and where they live now? Music? Education? Crime and violence? The economy? Clothing styles? The environment and power sources? Food and famine? Demographics?

Flexibility Skill Builder 2: Use Problem Solving Guidelines

The best way to encourage people to solve problems today in order to accommodate future trends is to show them how. If you act as a role model and solve problems effectively and with emotional intelligence, others will learn from your example.

> Paula owns a business that produces transfers for t-shirts. Sometimes her employees have personal problems such as an illness or death in the family. Just like she does with business problems, Paula listens and helps them work through their problems by exploring options. Then, Paula stays in touch with her employees and asks if things have gotten better. By her actions, Paula lets people know she cares about them.

Guidelines

Develop a standard process for problem-solving and train everyone on how to use it. The problem-solving process may be shared in the form of a poster, handouts or a booklet. The best problem-solving guidelines encourage people to use facts and feelings to develop solutions. For example, the state of the economy is influenced by present and anticipated natural disasters as well as consumer confidence.

Many problem-solving models include the following steps:

1. Clarify and analyze the problem. Find out what's making the problem happen. Be sure to consider facts as well as feelings when analyzing a problem.

2. Explore different options to solve the problem. Rarely is there just one solution to any problem. Use all parts of your brain to develop solutions—instincts, emotions, and logic.

3. Develop a plan of action to try out your solution. Plan to change work procedures as well as help people adjust to the changes.

4. Implement the plan in the real work environment.

5. Check results to see if the plan worked to solve the problem.

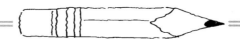

CHECK IN

Assess your organization's problem-solving strategies by responding to the following questions.

1. What problem-solving process or guidelines do you use?

_____

_____

_____

2. How well are the guidelines working?

_____

_____

_____

3. What does your company do to help employees use their emotional intelligence to solve problems?

_____

_____

_____

4. What changes to your problem-solving approach might be helpful?

_____

_____

_____

Strategy 5: Model and Encourage Emotional Control

Smart business communities encourage people to treat each other with respect and dignity. Smart business leaders are models of emotional control. They are calm and thoughtful when handling emotionally charged situations. Rudeness, hostility, and disrespect are not acceptable in a smart business community.

Disrespect lowers enthusiasm and reduces the ability to solve problems effectively.

Impact of Incivility

According to Christine M. Pearson, Professor of Management at Thunderbird School of Global Management, rude and discourteous behavior at work can be more harmful than many managers might expect. The bottom-line impact might be lost work time and lost effectiveness caused by worrying, trying to avoid the instigator, reduced commitment to the organization, decreased work effort, less time spent at work, and turnover.

Emotional Controller 1: Foster Civility

Take positive steps to reduce incivility and promote respect. Check (√) actions that may be helpful where you work.

- ❑ Make expectations clear. Involve employees in defining standards for civility and respect in their communication.

- ❑ State that hostile or offensive behavior will not be allowed.

- ❑ Have a discussion with new hires about standards and expectations at your company.

- ❑ Be sure that leaders model desired emotional and communication skills.

- ❑ Provide training on listening skills, how to give feedback, and how to manage stress and resolve conflicts.

- ❑ Spread the word by letting all employees know why preventing incivility is a priority.

- ❑ Let people know how to use civility in their day-to-day conduct.

- ❑ Give feedback to correct uncivil behavior.

- ❑ When a hostile event occurs, have a system for follow up.

- ❑ Encourage people who are treated uncivilly to report the situation.

Emotional Controller 2: Develop Civil Guidelines

An effective way to encourage civil communications is to actively involve associates in the design of guidelines. Following are examples of guidelines compiled from several workplaces.

Sample guidelines:

> ➤ We will show respect for others, partners, clients, co-workers, the community, and ourselves.

> ➤ We will give flexible choices to our customers and workers.

> ➤ We will leave personal problems at home.

> ➤ We will show appreciation to others especially when they help us.

> ➤ We will expect that our electronic communications respect people from all backgrounds, are clear, consistent with our corporate values, avoid negative religious references and omit offensive jokes.

CHECK IN

What does your organization do now to promote emotional control? Check (√) either "Yes" or "No."

	Yes	No
We have guidelines for civil communications.	☐	☐
We provide training on how to handle anger and conflict.	☐	☐
When people lose control of their emotions, we follow up by giving them helpful feedback and training.	☐	☐
We direct managers, supervisors, and executives to serve as models for how to express emotions.	☐	☐
We provide a process for helping a person who has been at the receiving end of rude behavior.	☐	☐
We conduct training about how to show respect to people from different cultures, backgrounds, and generations.	☐	☐
We provide instructions to employees on how to handle emotionally uncontrolled customers.	☐	☐

Strategy 6: Support Teamwork

Smart organizations help all associates feel they are on the same team. Teamwork is a strategy for serving customers smoothly and a way to develop new and better ideas for the future.

You may be a member of several types of teams. On whom do you depend to get your work done? Can you count on them to be supportive team members? Is your work team productive, creative, and collaborative?

A work team may be compared to an orchestra. The first time that musicians play together, they may sound out-of-tune and unpleasant. They need a score and conductor to keep everyone together. Each musician contributes to the total harmony of the orchestra. Beautiful music happens only after the entire orchestra practices together many times.

There is a difference between teams that have great performances and those that are "just okay." A great performance team is productive, reaches and exceeds goals, and helps the organization as well as the people who serve on the team. "Just okay" teams barely get their work done. "Just okay" teams get bogged down due to poor interpersonal communications, unclear roles, and low commitment.

High-performance team builders:

> ➤ Harmonize the ideas of all members so everyone can contribute in open and honest debate.

> ➤ Raise passion for shared goals so everyone plays "on the same page."

> ➤ Use team meeting time to build energy.

Team Builder 1: Harmonize Input

In *Emotional Intelligence*, Daniel Goleman says, "The key to a high group IQ is social harmony. It is this ability to harmonize that, all other things being equal, will make one group especially talented, productive, and successful, and another—with members whose talent and skill are equal in other regards—do poorly." As you review the following team characteristics, check (√) those that apply to your teams.

Mediocre teams have:

- ❑ **Closed communication.** Conversation may be guarded. There are hidden issues that everyone avoids. People give in to the person with the highest authority or the loudest voice.

- ❑ **Distrust.** People do not always take responsibility for carrying out tasks. Group members may be so brutally honest that they hurt each other's feelings. They constantly argue and try to outdo each other.

- ❑ **Sameness.** Everyone is similar in point-of-view, style, and background. They agree too easily without exploring options.

Great performance teams have:

- ❑ **Open communication.** Team members feel it is safe to express emotions. People know how to share their feelings in a positive and constructive way. They follow civil, respectful guidelines.

- ❑ **Trust.** They can rely on each other to follow through on promises. They can trust each other to be focused on goals rather than blaming others.

- ❑ **Variety.** Teams take advantage of different skills, communication styles, perspectives, and personalities.

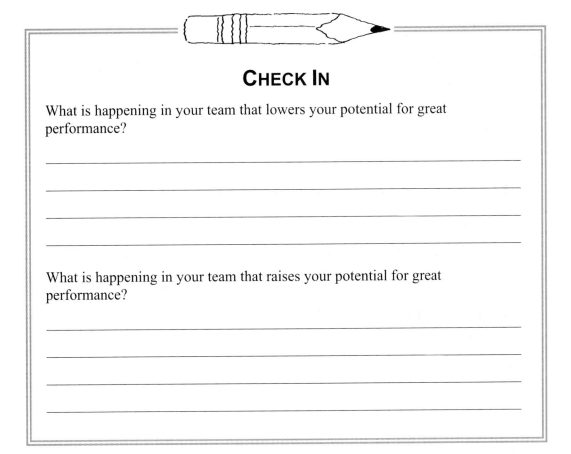

CHECK IN

What is happening in your team that lowers your potential for great performance?

_____

_____

_____

_____

What is happening in your team that raises your potential for great performance?

_____

_____

_____

_____

Increase Harmony in Your Team

A team goes from a healthy debate to open war when disagreement becomes a personal attack. Successful work teams discuss different opinions without becoming enemies. When people treat each other like enemies, their enthusiasm for teamwork declines. A work team becomes harmonious when debate is carried out without bad feelings. In a positive spirit of shared goals, everyone feels the process is fair and open. Everyone needs to have a shared concern for the organization rather than his or her narrow self-interest.

Ten communication behaviors contribute to social harmony. Use the following checklist at your next team meeting. Check the communications that your team uses. Discuss positive and negative examples.

Our team members:

- ❑ Use team guidelines that include listening to and respecting each other.
- ❑ Use a democratic and diversity-friendly process that enables everyone to speak.
- ❑ Take advantage of the skills and talents that each person brings to the team.
- ❑ Encourage everyone to express different opinions and points of view.
- ❑ Raise the "tough stuff" so it can be discussed openly.
- ❑ Avoid interrupting each other.
- ❑ Appreciate each other.
- ❑ Are as careful about what they say as how they say it.
- ❑ Focus on goals and not on making personal attacks.
- ❑ Use constructive rather than destructive criticism.

What communications guidelines would you like to use with your team? Write them down and share at your next meeting.

Team Builder 2: Conduct Diversity-Friendly Meetings

Use the following tips on how to conduct emotionally intelligent meetings that enable ALL team members to feel included and respected.

1. Know your audience including their language, ethnic and religious backgrounds, genders, disabilities and ages. For example, if necessary, schedule breaks around prayer times. Address people by name rather than pointing. In some cultures, pointing is considered rude and insulting.

2. When scheduling meetings and conferences, use a comprehensive calendar with major religious holidays. Understand observances including prayer times, food prohibitions, and fast days.

3. Provide options for food. Become educated about special food needs such as vegan, diabetic, halal, and kosher food requirements.

4. Prepare for emergencies especially for those with disabilities and different languages. Test routes prior to the meeting. Look for lighted and accessible exits, evacuation routes, audible and visible emergency warnings. Have assistants available to help those who will need it during and after the meeting for access to refreshments, rest rooms, entrances and exits.

5. Plan your physical environment. Make sure the aisles allow for mobility accessibility (space between aisles and tables). In some religions, men and women may prefer to sit separately. Provide opportunities for people to select their seating arrangements.

6. Use technology. Make sure your materials and audio visual aids work for all participants. Prepare your written resources in advance to have sufficient time for those with disabilities and/ or those who need language translation.

7. Have fun without offense. Require presenters to avoid disrespectful content, jokes, and language.

8. Develop meeting guidelines that show respect for all, that reflect your organization's values, focus discussion on content and outcomes rather than individual or group criticism.

9. Create a diverse planning committee to assist with all of these matters.

10. Use the following online resources:

➤ *Successful Meetings: The Diversity Factor* by Sondra Thiederman, PhD, Monster Contributing Writer. You've heard the phrase "Let's have a meeting" more times than you can count, right? That's because meetings are key to organizing projects, gathering information, and building relationships. Meetings can be productive and fun. They can also be frustrating or a waste of time. It all depends on the way people communicate. Diverse communication styles can make effective meetings more difficult to achieve, so it's important to remember these differences may result from divergent gender or cultural backgrounds. http://diversity.monster.com/articles/factor/

➤ Gestures: http://www.diversity-matters.net/publications-gestures.pdf

➤ Bridging the Generation Gap: http://www.diversity-matters.net/btgg0507.pdf

➤ Diversity-Friendly Meetings Survey Results: http://www.diversity-matters.net/nl07q1.pdf

Team Builder 3: Raise Passion

The best team members are enthusiastic, excited, energetic, and fascinated by their work most of the time. Mediocre team members are uninterested, unconcerned, unresponsive, disinterested, and pessimistic about their work most of the time. Use the "Passion Pressure Gauge" to measure your team's passion level. Circle the number that is nearest to the way people act about participating in the team.

High Passion   10   9   8   7   6   5   4   3   2   1   **Low Passion**

Ask your associates to use this gauge to assess themselves and others. Ask them to give you examples of how they show their passion. After comparing your rating to theirs, what did you learn about your team's enthusiasm?

Mediocre teams view teamwork as:

➤ An add-on to their "real" work

➤ A necessary but unpleasant requirement

➤ Something to get done as fast as possible

➤ A poor way to get work done

➤ Taking away from working alone

Great performance teams view teamwork as:

➤ An opportunity to get passionate about a challenging goal

➤ A way to work with other people so everyone can learn and grow

➤ Having fun

➤ Getting satisfaction from their work

➤ The best way to help each other **and** the customer

What Organizational Practices Foster Passion?

As you read the following list of organizational practices that raise passion, assess the suggested action steps. Are you doing them well or could you do better?

1. **What I do is important.**

   Example: A human resources manager for a national restaurant says, "The biggest thing is the feeling that I can make a difference to people and I feel important. I wouldn't be passionate if I couldn't make things better."

   Suggested Action Steps: Let people see how their efforts help people. Provide examples, results and real-life stories.

   ❑ I do well   ❑ I could do better

2. **My contributions are valued. My associates and customers appreciate me.**

   Example: The Director of Operations for a Bed and Breakfast tries to make everyone feel important whether a janitor or front-desk person.

   Suggested Action Steps: Give people positive feedback about their work. Let them hear what customers appreciate. Just say "thank you." Encourage and listen to their ideas.

   ❑ I do well   ❑ I could do better

3. **My work matches my personal values of helping others. There is no conflict between what I believe in and what my company does.**

   Example: The president of a neighborhood association says people have to identify with the task as if it were their own.

   Suggested Action Steps: Talk about company values and beliefs. Turn them into action. Let people see how the company values are part of everyday life.

   ❑ I do well   ❑ I could do better

4. **I have some degree of control over how I do my work. I know there are requirements.**

   Example: A counselor who helps individuals with disabilities get jobs enjoys her work. She manages her own time and sets priorities based on her workload.

   Suggested Action Steps: Give people opportunities to participate in making decisions and giving input. Give people control over the details of their work.

   ❑ I do well   ❑ I could do better

5. **I enjoy the people with whom I work including my co-workers and customers.**

   Example: The CEO of a community service organization says that the most important part of his work is the people he works with who keep him fired up.

   Suggested Action Steps: Create an enjoyable work environment. Use team meetings as an opportunity to get to know each other. Encourage people to help each other.

   ❑ I do well　　❑ I could do better

6. **Everyone treats me with respect. I appreciate being spoken to civilly and pleasantly.**

   Example: In one restaurant, the younger employees filed a complaint with their union because the managers yelled at the older employees.

   Suggested Action Steps: Be considerate of everyone. Be considerate of peoples' feelings, workspace and ideas. Have two-way conversations. Ask for help, don't yell or curse.

   ❑ I do well　　❑ I could do better

7. **My job uses my strengths and skills.**

   Example: Ray was stressed and exhausted at the end of the day. A friend discovered his natural talent for numbers. Ray started his own business as a bookkeeper for small businesses.

   Suggested Action Steps: Build on peoples' strengths. Help them to become better at their work by providing training and coaching. Give people opportunities for challenging work and promotions.

   ❑ I do well　　❑ I could do better

8. **I feel I am successful at my job.**

   Example: Nancy is an administrative assistant for a landfill business. She says proudly, "I have eight drivers working for ME! I am their boss. Can you believe that?"

   Suggested Action Steps: Help all associates to be successful. Tell them and show them how to be successful. Let people know what success is and let them know when they've accomplished it. Help them when they make mistakes.

   ❑ I do well　　❑ I could do better

CHECK IN

What are you doing now to raise passionate participation at your own organization?

_____

_____

_____

What are you doing that lowers passionate participation at your own organization?

_____

_____

_____

What do you believe are some action steps you might take to foster passionate teamwork?

_____

_____

_____

Build Energy at Team Meetings

Aside from doing day-to-day work tasks together, teams meet to generate new ideas, share information, solve problems, and communicate about everything that is important to serving their customers. Meetings may take place in person, via teleconference, or with web-based technology.

In the book, *Executive EQ: Emotional Intelligence in Leadership and Organizations*, authors Robert K. Cooper, Ph.D., and Ayman Sawaf suggest that you start every meeting by using an emotional check in. Ask three questions and rate your responses on a scale from 1 (low) to 10 (high). At the close of the meeting, ask similar questions to evaluate how well you did.

Meeting check-in

1. _____ How much energy do you feel right now?

2. _____ How open do you feel right now about new ideas and others' input?

3. _____ How do you rate your ability to focus on the meeting right now?

Meeting check-out

1. _____ How much energy do you feel now as the meeting is closing?

2. _____ How open do you feel you and everyone else was during the meeting?

3. _____ How well did everyone focus on the purpose of the meeting?

If you are leading the meeting, you may wish to find out what you can do to raise the energy, openness, and focus of the meetings. Ask yourself and your teammates, "What can I do to help others become more energetic, open, and focused during the meeting?"

If you are a participant, keep a record for yourself and look at your own behaviors during the meeting. Ask yourself, "What can I do to be more energetic, open, and focused during the meeting? How can I help others to be more enthusiastic?"

"Work Smart" Summary

An Action Plan for Using "Work Smart" People Strategies

Review the Work Smart Strategies for improving the organizational setting. Fill in action steps you will take to create a workplace in which people can think smart and be emotionally intelligent.

Strategy 1: Practice Organizational Self-Awareness

Practicing organizational self-awareness by using self-assessment, surveys, and other data-gathering tools to become aware of what your organization is doing to create a smart workplace.

The steps I plan to take to assess my organization are:

_____

_____

_____

_____

Strategy 2: Develop Social Skills

Developing social skills requires training people to communicate and relate well with others.

The steps I plan to take to develop associates' social skills at work are:

_____

_____

_____

_____

Strategy 3: Foster Optimism

Fostering optimism comes from:

➤ Helping people to see themselves in the organization's future

➤ Raising optimism by being positive, helping people to see their importance, and providing opportunities to make their own decisions

The steps I plan to take to foster optimism at work are:

_____

_____

_____

Strategy 4: Encourage Flexibility and Problem Solving

Encouraging flexibility depends on anticipating the future and finding options to solve problems. The steps I plan to take to encourage flexibility and problem solving at work are:

_____

_____

_____

Strategy 5: Model and Encourage Emotional Control

Modeling and encouraging people to control their emotions require civil communications guidelines. The steps I plan to take to enhance emotional control at work are:

_____

_____

_____

Strategy 6: Support Teamwork

Supporting teamwork depends on harmonizing input from everyone, increasing passion for the goal, and using team meetings to raise energy. The steps I plan to take to support teams at work are:

_____

_____

_____

A P P E N D I X

Recommended Reading

Books:

Barrett, Lisa Feldman. *The Wisdom in Feeling; Psychological Process in Emotional Intelligence*. New York, NY. Guilford Publications, Inc. 2002.

Benedict, Ruth. *The Chrysanthemum and the Sword; Patterns of Japanese Culture*. Boston, MA. Mariner Books by Houghton Mifflin, 1989.

Boas, Franz. *Rethinking Race: Franz Boas and his Contemporaries*. University Press of Kentucky, 1996.

Clifton, Donald O. and Paula Nelson. *Soar with Your Strengths*. New York, NY. Dell Books, 1996.

Cooper, Robert K. and Ayman Sawaf. *Executive EQ: Emotional Intelligence in Leadership and Organization*. New York, NY. Perigree, 1998.

Goleman, Daniel P. *Emotional Intelligence*. New York, NY. Bantam Books, 1997.

Goleman, Daniel P. *Social Intelligence: The New Science of Human Relationships*. New York, NY. Bantam Books, 2006.

Goleman, Daniel P. *Working with Emotional Intelligence*. New York, NY. Bantam Books, 2000.

Hockenbury, Don H. and Hockenbury, Sandra E. *Psychology*. New York, NY. Worth Publishers, 2006.

Kravitz, S. Michael. *Managing Negative People: Strategies for Success*. Crisp Series, 1995.

Pearsen, Christine. See list of books and research articles related to incivility. She is currently writing her fifth book, *Huh? Incivility, Its Causes, Costs and Cures*. http://www.thunderbird.edu/about_thunderbird/faculty_research/faculty_alphabetical/_189904_more.htm

Ryback, David. *Putting Emotional Intelligence to Work: Successful Leadership is More than IQ*. Boston, MA. Butterworth-Heinemann, 1997.

Salovey, Peter and David J. Sluyter, editors. *Emotional Development and Emotional Intelligence: Educational Implications*. New York, NY. Basic Books, 1997.

Sirkin, Harold, James Hemerling and Arindam Bhattacharya. *Globality: Competing With Everyone From Everywhere For Everything*. New York, NY. Grand Central Publishing, 2008.

Weisinger, Hendrie. *Emotional Intelligence at Work*. San Francisco, CA. Jossey-Bass, 2000.

Research articles:

Conflict Research Consortium, University of Colorado, USA. International Online Training Program On Intractable Conflict. Cultural Barriers to Effective Communication

http://www.colorado.edu/conflict/peace/problem/cultrbar.htm

Version 1.1.7 -- Revised July 20, 1999. Copyright © 1998-2005. A Project of the Conflict Research Consortium, Guy Burgess and Heidi Burgess, Co-Directors, Box 580, University of Colorado, Boulder, Colorado, 80309 USA.
Phone: (303) 492-1635
Fax: (303)492-2154
http://conflict.colorado.edu

Consortium for Research on Emotional Intelligence in Organizations, www.eiconsortium.org/

Elias, Maurice J., et al. "Promoting Social and Emotional Learning: Guidelines for Educators." Association for Supervision and Curriculum Development, 1997. www.ascd.org/books/eliasbook.html

NOTES

Books • Videos • Computer-Based Training Products

If you enjoyed this book, we have great news for you. There are more than 200 books available in the *Crisp Fifty-Minute™ Series*.

For more information visit us online at

www.axzopress.com

Subject Areas Include:
Management
Human Resources
Communication Skills
Personal Development
Sales/Marketing
Finance
Coaching and Mentoring
Customer Service/Quality
Small Business and Entrepreneurship
Training
Life Planning
Writing

VERQ